Solving Squirrel Problems

Books by Monte Burch

Ultimate Bass Boats
Field Dressing and Butchering Deer
Field Dressing and Butchering Upland Birds, Waterfowl, and Wild Turkeys
Field Dressing and Butchering Rabbits, Squirrels, and Other Small Game
Field Dressing and Butchering Big Game
The Field & Stream All-Terrain-Vehicle Handbook
Denny Brauer's Jig Fishing Secrets
Denny Brauer's Winning Tournament Tactics
Black Bass Basics
Guide to Calling & Rattling Whitetail Bucks
Guide to Successful Turkey Calling
Guide to Calling & Decoying Waterfowl
Guide to Successful Predator Calling
Pocket Guide to Seasonal Largemouth Bass Patterns
Pocket Guide to Seasonal Walleye Tactics
Pocket Guide to Old Time Catfish Techniques
Pocket Guide to Field Dressing, Butchering & Cooking Deer
Pocket Guide to Bowhunting Whitetail Deer
Pocket Guide to Spring & Fall Turkey Hunting
Guide to Fishing, Hunting & Camping Truman
The Pro's Guide to Fishing Missouri Lakes
Waterfowling: A Sportsman's Handbook
Modern Waterfowl Hunting
Shotgunner's Guide
Gun Care and Repair
Outdoorsman's Fix-It Book
Outdoorsman's Workshop
Building and Equipping the Garden and Small Farm Workshop
Basic House Wiring
Complete Guide to Building Log Homes
Children's Toys and Furniture
64 Yard and Garden Projects You Can Build
How to Build 50 Classic Furniture Reproductions
The Indoors and Out
The Home Cabinetmaker
How to Build Small Barns & Outbuildings
Masonry & Concrete
Pole Building Projects
Building Small Barns, Sheds & Shelters
Home Canning & Preserving (with Joan Burch)
Building Mediterranean Furniture (with Jay Hedden)
Fireplaces (with Robert Jones)
The Homeowner's Complete Manual of Repair and Improvement (with three others)
The Good Earth Almanac Series
Survival Handbook
Old-Time Recipes
Natural Gardening Handbook

Solving Squirrel Problems

How to Keep This Ubiquitous Pest Out of Home and Garden

Monte Burch

THE LYONS PRESS
Guilford, Connecticut
An imprint of The Globe Pequot Press

The Lyons Press is an imprint of The Globe Pequot Press.

10 9 8 7 6 5 4 3 2 1

Printed in the United States of America

Designed by Compset, Inc.

ISBN 1–58574–673–8

Library of Congress Cataloging-in-Publication data is available on file.

Contents

Introduction   vii

Chapter 1: Understanding Squirrels   1

Chapter 2: Bird Feeder Raiders   35

Chapter 3: Lawns, Gardens, and Flowers   67

Chapter 4: Squirrels in the Orchard   87

Chapter 5: Squirrels in Houses, Barns, and
        Outbuildings   93

Chapter 6: Other Rodent Pests   107

Chapter 7: Lethal Versus Nonlethal   129

Chapter 8: Hunting Squirrels   153

Chapter 9: Squirrel Stew, Pot Pie, and
        Other Goodies   179

Chapter 10: Squirrels, the Good Guys   213

Sources   229

Introduction

S quirrels—some folks love 'em, some folks hate 'em. You may love them because they are fun to watch. Their antics as they scramble acrobatically through the trees, tight-walk power lines, nimbly jump from one aerial object to another, or scamper over the ground foraging for nuts and seeds can provide great entertainment for young and old alike.

But you may hate them, too. As with many wildlife species, squirrels can become nuisances. They will quickly take over a backyard bird feeder. They are notorious for raiding gardens and orchards. And, in some instances, they can create health or home safety problems, especially if they get into attics or any other home spaces.

A wide variety of techniques for solving nuisance squirrel problems, both nonlethal and lethal, are described in this book. Nonlethal methods include utilizing repellents or deterrents for nuisance squirrels. Other nonlethal methods involve live trapping and relocation. Lethal methods include killer traps, poisons, shooting, and hunting. Also discussed is when to call in a nuisance-animal contractor.

Hunting squirrels, where allowed, is a time-honored tradition and a great way of keeping their numbers under control. Hunting tactics, and even squirrel recipes, are also included.

For those who enjoy the antics of squirrels, information on attracting them is provided as well.

As a bonus, information on controlling other nuisance rodents, such as chipmunks, rats, mice, gophers, and even groundhogs, is also included.

Don't let nuisance squirrels drive you crazy. Learn how to solve your squirrel problems.

Understanding Squirrels

Before you can combat the enemy, you must know it. An understanding of squirrels can go a long way in determining if you have a nuisance squirrel problem, and how best to solve it.

Squirrels have a long and large family tree (pun intended). Squirrels belong to the rodent (Rodentia) order, the largest of the fourteen orders of mammals, which has thirty-one families,

Understanding the habits of squirrels is the key to solving squirrel problems.

including tree squirrels (Sciuridae), ground squirrels (Sper-mophilus), flying squirrels (Glaucomys), marmots (Marmota), and chipmunks (Tamias). The scientific Latin family name "Sci-uridae" actually comes from a Greek term meaning "shadow tail." The squirrel families have around 250 different species, including tree squirrels, ground and flying squirrels, marmots, prairie dogs, and woodchucks. All have five toes on their rear feet and four on their front. Some have hairy tails, some quite bushy. These rodents are chewers, or more correctly, gnawers. All rodents have long, curved, chisel-shaped incisor teeth in the front of both the upper and lower jaws. These teeth grow continually throughout the life of the rodent.

Rodents must gnaw or chew in order to keep teeth growth in check. The incisor teeth of squirrels grow about six inches each year. They have a hard outer coating of enamel with a softer material on the back. This produces a sharp "chisel" tooth. There's no nut too tough for a squirrel to crack, or more correctly, to

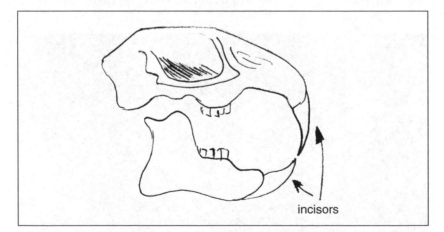

incisors

Members of the rodent family, squirrels have long, curved upper and lower teeth that continually grow, requiring constant gnawing or chewing.

gnaw through. Once they get the nut open, squirrels use their molars in a side-to-side grinding action to chew their food. Woodchucks and marmots have white incisors; all others have yellow.

Tree Squirrels

Tree or arboreal squirrels do not have cheek pouches as do the ground squirrels. Although they spend the majority of their time in trees, they also forage on the ground. They do not hibernate, but store their food in holes in the ground, tree cavities, and even holes or openings in buildings. Their diet includes a wide variety of nuts, fruits, berries, seeds, twigs, buds, bark, fungi, and also insects. In fact, there's little they won't eat in these categories, and they're extremely efficient foragers— the reason they often become nuisances. Once they discover a food source, they'll stay on it and become extremely inventive in continuing to utilize that source. Tree squirrels usually nest in cavities in trees. If they find openings in houses or other buildings, they may nest in attics and any other open spaces. In the warmer months they often spend time in leaf nests built in the canopies of trees.

Litters run from one to seven and arboreal squirrels can have from one to two litters per year. Gestation is from forty to forty-five days. The young are born blind and naked. First litters are normally born in late spring or early summer. Several years ago, during a logging operation on our farm, we discovered a litter in December, which is fairly unusual.

Several varieties of arboreal or tree squirrels exist. These include the fox (*Sciurus niger*); eastern gray (*Sciurus carolinensis*); red (*Tamiasciurus hudsonicus*), also known as the chickaree or pine squirrel; flying squirrels (*Glaucomys spp.*); California or western gray (*Sciurus griseus*); Arizona gray (*Sciurus arizonensis*);

the tassel-eared squirrel of the West (*Sciurus aberti*); and a sub-species of the tassel-eared squirrel, the Kaibab squirrel. The most common squirrels, and those that cause the most prob-lems, however, are the fox and eastern gray squirrels.

Eastern Gray Squirrels (*Sciurus carolinensis*)

At least half a dozen subspecies of gray squirrels have a range from the southern edge of Canada to the Gulf and then across the entire eastern portion of the United States. The body of the adult gray squirrel is about eight to ten inches long, with the bushy tail about another eight to ten inches. The fur is silvery or salt-and-pepper gray on the upper body. The fur on the under-side ranges from whitish to a very pale gray, or sometimes a pale cream color with white below. It has a light yellowish or tan eye ring and muzzle. The backs of the ears are also light. The gray is the only tree squirrel with a white-bordered tail. Black and even white varieties are also seen, although they are not common. I've also seen several gray and white mixed or piebald-colored squirrels.

The little grays are nimble and graceful creatures with more pointed noses than the bigger fox squirrels. Weighing about a pound, or slightly less in the South, where they are often called "cat" squirrels, the grays are true acrobats who will amuse you with their antics. Their habits are similar to those of a cat. They are extremely playful, chasing each other around and over trees. They also groom themselves like cats, licking and using their claws to clean and fluff their fur. Gray squirrels tend to be early risers, often leaving their nest at first light and foraging through sunrise and a bit after. Then they retire to their nest, or slumber away on a limb or other high platform. Late in the afternoon they awaken and make another foraging trek.

The little gray squirrel, a creature of the hardwood forests, river and creek bottoms, as well as city parks and suburban yards, is a nimble acrobat.

The habitat of the gray squirrel is primarily hardwood forests, river and creek bottoms, and, of course, city parks and suburbia. Gray squirrels have also been introduced in some western city parks. Their primary food is mast, although they eat buds and fruits when available. Although biologists have identified seventy-six different foods squirrels eat, the most important are the buds, nuts, and fruits of pecan, oak, hickory, walnut, elm, and mulberry trees. If a community has numerous mast trees, the grays will be in abundance. During the early years of settling the country, when there were vast hardwood forests, grays were extremely numerous. In times when specific areas

The Range of the Eastern Gray Squirrel

The Range of the Western Gray Squirrel

would have a mast crop failure, large numbers of grays would migrate to other areas. These migrations would often run through towns as well as across country. In many instances grays may still migrate to find food sources.

The importance of mast as a food is indicated by the drastic fluctuation that can occur in gray squirrel numbers. A good mast crop is especially important in the wintertime when the females are gestating. In years of good nut crops, a greater number of squirrels are born. In years of poor nut crops, the population drops.

Gray squirrels can live to about fifteen years of age. They make several sounds, including soft mews, a chattering of teeth, and the *chirrrrrrrring* scold, as any woods traipser will recall. They also make a sharp barking sound. Gray squirrels flick their tails sharply, as if irritated.

Fox Squirrel (*Sciurus niger*)

About ten subspecies of fox squirrels are found distributed from the Dakotas down through Nebraska, Kansas, and into central Texas, then over much of the East, except for the extreme northern portions of the eastern states. Fox squirrels tend to be larger than grays, weighing from one to three pounds. Their total length can run from twenty to twenty-nine inches. They're usually slightly orange, or red-fox colored, with lighter yellow on their undersides. The upper colors can, however, vary a great deal, from a dark brown to lighter red. Different regions tend to have somewhat different colors, with the squirrels found in the Northeast a salt-and-pepper coloring of the gray, but with some red mixed in. A more rusty red color is found in the midwestern and western squirrels. Melanism or black coloring also occurs in the fox species. Most black fox

Fox squirrels are bigger than grays and are more adaptable in habitat, often living in farm fencerows, small wood lots, as well as city parks and backyards.

squirrels are found in the South. Some may also have white mixed in with white tail ends and white faces.

The habitat of fox squirrels overlaps somewhat that of the gray, with similar foods. For the most part, however, fox squirrels are found in the higher ridges of timberland. They're also more adaptable as to habitat. In the South, they are found in the coniferous woods of long-leaf pine and around the borders of cypress swamps. In the Midwest, fox squirrels inhabit woodlots, timbered fencerows, and draws. They are also commonly found in Osage orange hedgerows, once very numerous, but quickly becoming a thing of the past. The "hedge balls" or fruits of these trees are also typical winter foods of prairie fox squirrels. They gnaw the fruits apart to get to the seeds inside.

Fox squirrels also don't seem to have the early-rising habits of grays. They tend to leave their nest a bit later and are more

The Range of the Fox Squirrel

active through the middle of the day, retiring back to their nest earlier than the gray squirrels as well. Fox squirrels are also more adaptable when it comes to foods. They will raid a cornfield, fruit orchard, or garden with the best of the animal pests, quickly becoming nuisances.

Fox squirrels produce a sharp barking and shrill chatter, as well as chatter their teeth. They tend to produce a slower tail movement than grays, waving it when irritated. They have a life expectancy of about ten years.

Red Squirrel (*Tamiasciurus hudsonicus*)

Red squirrels are predominantly found in evergreen forests, and are the most common species in the upper North woods. They are smaller than either fox or gray squirrels, usually from

The Range of the Red Squirrel

seven to eight inches in length with five- to six-inch tails. They're predominantly reddish, but occasionally tend more toward a lighter orange coloring. Their backs may have some dark brown or dark red and their tails have a buff border. In the summer their sides have a black line, but in the winter the coloring is paler. Red squirrels also have ear tufts.

Red squirrels are found mostly in the evergreen or coniferous forests, with fewer numbers found in hardwoods or deciduous forests. One of the most common signs is a scattering of cuttings from pinecones left on logs, stumps, and rocks. Red squirrels tend to cache or store food in piles under logs and rock piles, and in hollows in trees and logs. They do not bury individual nuts as do the fox and gray squirrels. Their life expectancy is nine years. Red squirrels twitch their tails and bodies, and give a loud, scolding chatter.

Douglas Squirrel (*Tamiasciurus douglasii*)

The Douglas squirrel is found primarily in the coniferous forests of the Northwest. A rather small squirrel with a seven-inch body and four- to six-inch tail, it is also called the chickaree or pine squirrel. In some parts of the North it is often mistaken for the red squirrel since its coloring is very similar. The upper body runs from brown to a gray-brown with the sides running more to a dark red or auburn coloring. In summer a distinct black line is found on the sides, but the line is not evident in winter. The color of the underside runs from reddish orange with black guard hairs to a dirty gray. The tail is reddish, with a black border and white-tipped edge hairs. In the winter long hairs are found on the tips of the ears.

The Douglas squirrel is found primarily in the forests of the Northwest, and is also called the chickaree or pine squirrel.

The Range of the Douglas Squirrel

Western Gray Squirrel (*Sciurus griseus*)

The western gray squirrel is found from central Washington down into western Oregon and in much of California, except for the desert regions. The western gray is about a foot in length, with another foot in a long, extremely bushy tail. Its upper coloring runs from light to dark gray with creamy white or light gray underparts. Distinguishing marks include a white belly and dark feet.

Nayarit Squirrel (*Sciurus nayaritensis*)

The Nayarit squirrel is found in southwestern New Mexico. A subspecies of the gray squirrel, the Nayarit squirrel has a reddish coloring.

Abert's Squirrel (*Sciurus aberti*)

Two tassel-eared squirrels are found in Arizona, New Mexico, and Colorado. The Abert's squirrel is a very colorful creature and fairly large with a body ranging to a foot in length and an eight- to nine-inch tail. Its upper coloring is dark gray with a grizzled appearance and its sides range from dark gray to black with a middle stripe of dark brown. Its tail may be either white on the underside, with the white extending to the sides, or all white. The under coloring can be white or black. The Abert's most distinctive features are its black ear tufts.

Two tassel-eared squirrels are found in the West. They include the Abert's and Kaibab. Shown here is the Abert's.

The Range of the Abert's Squirrel

Map of Abert's squirrel population. Kaibab squirrels are found only in the higher elevations.

The Kaibab tassel-eared squirrel (*Sciurus aberti kaibabensis*) is found primarily north of the Grand Canyon. Its coloration, size, and habits are similar to those of the Abert's squirrel, but it has an all-white tail.

Flying Squirrels

Two flying squirrels are also included in the tree squirrel species. These include the southern and northern flying squirrels. Both species have a loose fold of skin reaching along their sides from their rear feet to their front feet. Flying squirrels do not actually fly, but rather glide from one place to another. Sev-

Flying squirrels become nuisances. They love to nest in attics and are often nocturnal.

eral years ago I was fishing on Truman Reservoir in central Missouri, which at the time still had lots of standing timber. As my bass boat bumped a tree, out came a flying squirrel from a hole in the top. The creature eyed me for a second or two, then jumped into the air and glided about thirty feet to another tree. It was a rare meeting, because these squirrels are primarily nocturnal animals. To see the graceful glide in daylight was a real treat.

Southern Flying Squirrel (*Glaucomys volans*)

Southern flying squirrels are fairly small squirrels, reaching only about ten inches in total length with a six-inch body. Their

The Range of the Southern Flying Squirrel

fur is thick and luxurious, including along the edges of the side skin folds, and their coloring ranges from a dark olive-brown on the upper parts to white on the under parts. Their tail is flatter than that of other tree squirrels. Due to their nocturnal nature, flying squirrels' eyes are quite large. They tend to sleep away the day in tree cavities and are also fond of finding openings into buildings and will nest or sleep in attics and other locations. They're found primarily in older, mature woods with tall trees and lots of tree cavities. With the right take-off location, flying squirrels can glide long distances, as far as 125 feet. Flying squirrels are also more gregarious than other squirrel species. They tend to group together, especially in their sleeping quarters, where their numbers may range up to several dozen all in one spot. Flying squirrels don't make the irritated chattering or barking of other tree squirrels. Instead, they tend to make chirping, twittering, birdlike sounds.

The Range of the Northern Flying Squirrel

Northern Flying Squirrel (*Glaucomys sabrinus*)

The northern flying squirrel is similar to the southern, except larger. It also has a different under coloring with the hairs light gray at the base.

The habitat of the northern flying squirrel is primarily conifers, but it's sometimes found in mixed coniferous and deciduous forests. The northern flying squirrel has only one litter per year.

Similar Habits of Tree Squirrels

Most species of tree squirrels have similar habits. Their winter home is normally in a leafy nest located in a cavity of a tree or other object. Older trees, particularly white oaks, sycamores, elms, and soft maples, provide favored cavities for wintering

Most tree squirrels nest or den in hollow cavities in trees.

and as nurseries. These nests provide snug and safe protection from the weather as well as enemies. Summer nests are leaf nests built in the tops of large trees. These nests consist of a rough twig framework with leaves layered over the frame. The squirrel then burrows into the leaf mass to create a hollow area in the center. You can often get a good idea of the squirrel population by the number of leafy nests easily seen in deciduous forests in late winter. This number can, however, be misleading since some squirrels, particularly the boar squirrels, may have more than one nest.

The common distribution of gray squirrels covers most of the eastern part of the United States and the Southeast. Fox squirrels have a bit more westerly range although similar to that of the grays. Both species tend to live their entire lives within

Tree squirrels commonly use leaf nests, especially during the warm season months.

200 yards of their home and usually don't travel very far from the vicinity of their preferred trees, with the exception of the gray squirrels' migration for food sources.

Gray squirrels mate in late December and through January. Gestation is about forty-five days and the majority of litters are born in February through March. Fox squirrels usually begin breeding a week or two before the grays. In late May through July another mating period occurs.

Young squirrels are born hairless and have their eyes and ears closed. They do, however, possess well-developed claws. About six to seven weeks after birth, the young squirrels come out of the nest for the first time. In about another week or so they are weaned.

One of the most curious squirrel habits is that of burying nuts in the ground, which both gray and fox squirrels do. It appears the buried nuts are not an individual cache; the entire squirrel community shares in the stash. Biologists suggest the general location of this stored food is found to some degree by some limited memory sense. Individual nuts, however, are probably more often found by smell. Yet not every nut is dug up—many of the unrecovered ones sprout and eventually become trees. In that aspect, squirrels are great little foresters.

Anyone who has tromped the woods in wintertime after a snow will see the evidence of squirrels digging in the ground for their buried food sources. Squirrels also store nuts and seeds in other places, including tree cavities, rock and wood piles, and even cavities or holes in buildings.

I'll never forget a squirrel encounter with the first snowstorm of the year in Missouri several years ago. Overnight we re-

Squirrels store caches of nuts, burying them in the ground or, in the case of ground squirrels, hiding them in rock piles or tree cavities.

ceived about ten inches of extremely wet snow. Sitting in my tree stand while hunting deer the next morning, I watched a squirrel peek tentatively out of his hole, scurry down the tree, and jump to the ground. He instantly exploded out of the snow, dropped back down, exploded out again a couple more times, and then scampered back up to a tree limb, where he seemed to be pondering the problem. He made another tentative try, and then scurried back up the tree and into his warm nest. I was laughing so hard I missed seeing a nice buck.

Seasonal Squirrel Foods

Squirrels are omnivorous—they'll actually eat both plant and animal matter—but their primary diet is plant food. Following is a seasonal look at the most common food utilized by fox and gray squirrels.

Squirrels are omnivorous—they'll eat both plant and animal matter—but their primary diet is plant foods.

- *Early Spring*
  Buds and flowers of deciduous trees, particularly the elms, maples, oaks, and sweet gum.
- *Late Spring/Early Summer*
  Mushrooms, mulberries, berry crops, wild cherries, pokeberries, and wild strawberries.
- *Summer*
  Corn in the milk stage, both sweet and field corn, leafy portions of herbaceous plants, wild plums, and grapes.

Nuts, such as hickories, acorns, walnuts, and hazelnuts, are the preferred foods during the fall and are buried to carry the squirrels through the winter months.

- *Fall*
  Hickory and hazelnuts are first, followed by pecans, walnuts, beechnuts, and acorns. Also the fruits of honey locust and sugar maple trees.
- *Winter*
  Buried acorns or nuts are the staple that carries squirrels through the winter months. Hedge balls, the fruits of Osage orange trees, are also highly utilized.

Squirrel Sign

Squirrels bound, or scamper when on the ground, regardless of whether the ground is covered with snow or bare. They hop like rabbits from place to place, leaving a very distinctive track pattern. The pattern is about four inches in length with the rear

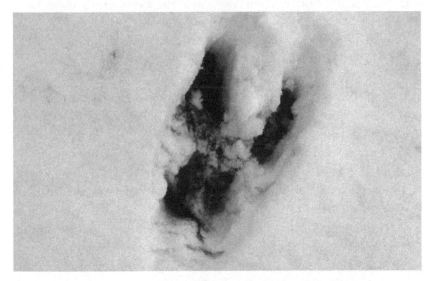

Squirrel sign includes droppings, tracks, and evidence of gnawing.

feet positioned in front of the front feet. The pattern of squirrel tracks is about eighteen to twenty inches apart. The droppings are about one-quarter inch in diameter and three-eighths inch long, and are tapered.

Other signs of squirrels are the leavings from their nut cuttings. The squirrels gnaw the outer shells of walnuts, acorns, hickories, and other nuts to get at the nutmeats. The ground below a large tree with abundant mast will often be littered with gnawed nutshells. Deer also relish these nuts. Deer, however, tend to bite through them, leaving sharp teeth marks instead of gnawed areas. I love hickory nut pie, but squirrels love hickories as much as I do, and they always seem to beat me to the best trees. The fox squirrels in my neighborhood beat me to the hazelnuts as well.

A tiny worm is often found in many hickory nuts and the evidence is a very tiny hole in the outer shell. I haven't figured it out yet, but I've never seen a wormy nut even nibbled on by a squirrel.

Squirrel Senses

Squirrels have very keen senses—one of the reasons they've lasted so long. The ancestors of today's bushytail have been traced back as far as fifty million years, during the Miocene era.

Their sense of smell is very important. Biologists say squirrels find buried nuts and other foods primarily by their keen sense of smell. Considering these food sources are often buried under leaves, a few inches of soil, and oftentimes snow and ice, this is truly remarkable. Biologists also suggest squirrels can smell the difference between the "good" and "bad" nuts, which would explain why they quickly discard nuts with worms inside. Or, they may eat the interloper as well.

As with many other mammals, squirrels are territorial. And, like most mammals, they use urine, combined with other scents, for instance from oil glands, to mark their territory. Females in estrus also provide the scent trails needed to attract males.

Squirrel hearing is not as acute as some other animals', and they don't depend as greatly on this sense. Note that they do not have forward facing, easily swiveling ears, such as deer's. The ears can, however, swivel to some degree, which aids in detecting distant noises. The ears are well covered in fur, with squirrels in the North having ear tufts for more protection in the cold.

When it comes to sight, squirrels are right up there at the top of the list. Their eyes, like those of other prey species such as rabbits and deer, are situated on either side of their head, and slightly forward—"all the better to see you with, my dear."

Squirrel Anatomy

Although born naked, squirrels develop their fur coats in about two weeks. Adult squirrels are covered with fur, including fur on the bottoms of the feet of some species for protection from the cold in the winter. The fur is multi-layered with the thick inner fur providing insulation. Longer hairs, called "guard hairs," are intermixed. These provide the primary coloring of squirrels and may be of several colors on an individual squirrel. It's thought these guard hair colors are developed as a natural camouflage.

Squirrels molt or lose their hair twice a year, in the spring and then again in the fall. In addition to the normal coloring of the different species, melanistic or black squirrels and true albino or white squirrels also exist.

All squirrels also have specialized tactile hairs or whiskers called "vibrissae." These hairs stick out on either side of their faces and provide information on their surroundings in holes and tunnels. Four sets of these tactile hairs are arranged with the main group on either side of the nose, one set under the chin, one set above the eyes, and one set below the eyes. Each nipple of the female squirrels also has one tactile hair. Tactile hairs are also located just above the wrists on the forepaws.

Tree squirrels are most easily identified by their tails. Squirrel tails are very important, as they provide balance when leaping and running. Their tails also act somewhat as parachutes when they fall, providing some control. Flying squirrel tails are flattened to provide even more glide control. Squirrels also wrap their bodies with their long bushy tails to provide protection against the cold. And last, their tails are used for communica-

Squirrels communicate in many ways, including sounds, scent, and body language, such as flicking their tails.

tion. A squirrel holding its tail motionless indicates that it is re-
laxed, while one flicking its tail rapidly indicates that it is excited
or scared. The flicking tail also communicates danger to other
squirrels in the area. The squirrel's tail may also act as a decoy to
predators, allowing the squirrel to escape missing only a bit of a
body part instead of becoming food for an owl or other predator. I've seen more than one squirrel with part of its tail missing.

The feet of tree squirrels are highly adapted to their life in
the treetops. All four feet have formidable claws. Baby squirrels
are born with their claws. The hind legs are very flexible, allowing the squirrels to rotate their hind feet and hook their claws
in a wide variety of positions. This allows them to even feed up-
side down while eating with their front claws.

Squirrel Predators

The most common cause of death is not predators, but a lack of
food or severe cold weather—both often combined with parasites or infections. The automobile, however, may be the squirrel's most dangerous predator. In fact, some biologists measure
squirrel populations in well-populated areas by "road kill."
Squirrels also often get into trouble looking for water to drink.
I've fished several dead squirrels from my cattle watering tanks,
especially when the water has gotten low in the tank. The squirrels jump in, but can't climb back out. They're also notorious
for drowning in swimming pools as well. Humankind is and has
been one of the top predators of squirrels, whether hunting for
food or attempting to control nuisance squirrels. In addition to
humans, their pets are also a common danger to squirrels. Domestic cats and dogs readily attack young squirrels. Adult squirrels can usually take care of themselves with most household
pets. My Irish setter hates squirrels with a passion, decided by a

definite losing match with a big fat fox squirrel when she was a young puppy.

In addition to humans and their pets, squirrels have a number of natural predators as well. Their own kind provides a danger, especially to baby or young squirrels. Both females and males will prey on baby or young squirrels. Great horned owls are probably their most feared predators. They prey on both young and adults, but fortunately, their foraging is primarily at night, when most squirrels are home in bed. Hawks also quite frequently prey on young squirrels. Raccoons, martins, and weasels get into squirrel dens and prey on baby and young squirrels. Foxes, coyotes, and bobcats, as well as ground-dwelling snakes, also prey on squirrels, primarily young or weakened squirrels.

Squirrels can live for a decade, but most don't live more than five years in the wild. Only about 25 percent survive their first year.

Although the automobile may be the squirrel's most dangerous predator, it also has other predators, including owls and hawks.

Ground Squirrels, Chipmunks, and Marmots

Ground squirrels have internal cheek pouches. They do not have striped faces as do the chipmunks. Ground squirrels dig burrows, and in their northern ranges they hibernate through the winter months. Omnivorous, their food includes seeds, fruits, and plants as well as insects, small mammals, and birds. They commonly have only one litter a year, except for the rock squirrel. The young are born blind and naked, but are weaned in about a month. Some species may have more than a dozen in a litter.

Thirteen-Lined Ground Squirrel (*Spermophilus tridecemlineatus*)

The thirteen-lined ground squirrel is the most widely spread ground squirrel with a range that covers much of the central United States up into Canada and down through Texas. This is the only striped ground squirrel. Its length is from four and a half to

Ground squirrels and chipmunks, although "cute," can also become problems for homeowners.

six and a half inches with a tail running to five inches. Coloration is light to dark brown with thirteen stripes running the length of the body. The top stripe is broken into spots and the under coloring is white. Its favored habitat is brushy wood edges, grassy roadsides, prairies, backyards, and golf courses. The ground squirrel runs with its tail straight out behind and is often seen scurrying across roads. It produces a high-pitched *chirrrrring* sound.

Spotted Ground Squirrel (*Spermophilus spilosoma*)

A fairly small squirrel, the spotted ground squirrel ranges from five to six inches with a tail up to three and a half inches. The only spotted ground squirrel, its coloration is a light reddish or gray brown with square-shaped spots on the back. Under coloration is white and the tail is not bushy. Range and habitat is the semiarid plains of the Southwest.

Franklin's Ground Squirrel (*Spermophilus franklinii*)

The Franklin's ground squirrel is one of the largest ground squirrels, with a nine- to ten-inch body and six-inch tail. It is also the darkest with a dark gray to brown coloration blending to slightly lighter on the undersides. The Franklin's ground squirrel has no stripes or spots and is also called the gray gopher. Its range is primarily in the northern Midwest into Canada and its favored habitat is pastures, fields, and woodland edges. This ground squirrel is a tree climber, but lives in well-hidden burrows and makes a whistling, birdlike sound.

Rock Squirrel (*Spermophilus variegatus*)

Found primarily in rocky areas, the rock squirrel likes to sit on top of a boulder, but can also climb trees and bushes. Its range is from Colorado down through New Mexico and Arizona, and into some parts of Idaho and Nevada. A large squirrel with a ten- to eleven-inch body, the rock squirrel also has a long, ten-inch bushy tail. Coloration is variegated, blending gray and brown, with lighter coloration below. The head and back are sometimes black. The rock squirrel produces a loud whistling sound.

Richardson's Ground Squirrel (*Spermophilus richardsonii*)

A fairly large squirrel, but not quite as large as the Franklin's, the Richardson's ground squirrel ranges from eight to nine and a half inches in body length with a tail about four and a half inches. Its coloration is a dark gray above with pale gray below, and there are no spots. The tail is a light brown with a light tan or white border. Its range is the upper West into Canada and east to Minnesota and its favored habitat is sagebrush, pastures, and prairies. The Richardson's ground squirrel makes a shrill, birdlike sound.

Eastern Chipmunk (*Tamias striatus*)

The eastern chipmunk is a small squirrel, ranging from five to six inches in body length with a tail to four inches. Its coloration is reddish brown on upper portions to white on the underside with stripes on its face, back, and sides. Its rump does not have stripes and is a reddish brown. Its favored habitat is pastures, edges of hardwood forests, rock piles, rock fences, and rock walls as well as outbuildings. One of the more unsocial ground squirrels, the eastern chipmunk sits upright, runs with its tail up, and makes a variety of sharp and soft *clucks* and *chirps*. Eastern chipmunks are also frequenters of campgrounds and picnic areas, where they steal bits of food.

Least Chipmunk (*Eutamias minimus*)

Ranging from three and a half to four and a half inches in body length and with a tail to four and a half inches, the least chipmunk is a very small squirrel. Its coloration is varied from reddish brown to gray with stripes on the back, face, and sides. The stripes extend to the base of the tail. The least chipmunk prefers openings in coniferous forests, mixed woodlands, woods edges, rock piles, and outbuildings.

Yellow-Bellied Marmot (*Marmota flaviventris*)

The yellow-bellied marmot is found in the Northwest to the edge of South Dakota and down to the edge of New Mexico and to lower California. The marmot is a large squirrel that can reach up to ten pounds in weight. It has a body ranging from fourteen to nineteen inches and a tail up to nine inches in length. Its upper parts are yellowish brown with some gray mixed in, and its neck is also yellowish. Its face is black with white between the eyes. The under parts are yellow with feet ranging from light to dark brown. Its favored habitat is the rocks of the western mountains.

Woodchuck (*Marmota monax*)

The largest of the squirrel family, woodchucks, also called groundhogs, range in size from sixteen to twenty inches, with a tail up to seven inches in length. Woodchucks can weigh more than ten pounds, their body is short and squat, and the ears and tail are small. Their coloration ranges from a dark to yellowish brown with some gray mixed in above. Unlike the marmot, there is no white between the eyes. Under body parts are somewhat lighter, and the feet are black. Their habitat is varied, from brush and dozer piles to rocky piles and brushy fencerows, always near open fields or pastures. They often frequent mowed roadsides but favor fields of alfalfa and clovers. They're most active early in the morning and then again in late afternoon. Woodchucks can both swim and climb. They dig intricate burrows, often with more than one entrance. These burrows can cause problems for farmers and undermine building foundations. Woodchucks hibernate in a ground den through the winter. They make a very sharp whistle, and for that reason are also sometimes called "whistle pigs."

Dangers of Squirrels

Although some members of the squirrel family seem like adorable little creatures, especially the ground squirrels and chipmunks, don't make the mistake of thinking they're not dangerous. All have very sharp teeth and claws and can bite and scratch worse than an irritated tomcat. And, they fight like crazy when cornered. More than one family dog has learned this lesson the hard way.

Squirrels can often have external as well as internal parasites. They're frequently infected with fleas, a problem for humans if they learn to inhabit dwellings. They're also susceptible to ticks. Squirrels taken in some areas in the summer months, before a hard freeze, are often covered with them. Lice and mites are also common to squirrels. Another external parasite is the botfly larva, especially in the South. Botfly larvae burrow under the skin, creating open sores. Squirrels can also contract Shope's fibroma, or rabbit horn, a viral wart growth. Weakened or malnourished squirrels may also contract mange, most commonly in the late winter.

Internal parasites may include worms, and squirrels can carry some diseases transmittable to humans. These include typhus and encephalitis, as well as sylvatic plague, transmitted through fleas. Squirrels can also carry and transmit rabies. If at any time you have to handle squirrel carcasses, especially those that appear to have died from a disease, make sure you wear rubber gloves and dispose of the gloves properly.

Squirrels can and do attack other animals. They can be a danger to pets, especially smaller ones. They'll also attack small birds. Even humans are not safe from these seemingly friendly creatures. This is especially so in urban parks and on college campuses with large, old, and well-tended nut trees that afford both food and shelter for numerous squirrels. Then there's the problem of hand-feeding. In many of these places people hand-feed the squirrels. Once squirrels lose their fear of humans, they, like any wild animal, can become serious threats. Once they learn humans mean food, they will often attack in an attempt to take it, especially if it is not offered to them. More than one picnicker has watched their French fries disappear to a hungry squirrel. And children are often bitten when they try to pet a "tame" squirrel. These bites can be extremely severe due to the sharp teeth and quickness of the animal, and also cause serious infections.

2

Bird Feeder Raiders

Feeding birds is one of America's favorite hobbies. Hundreds of thousands of people feed them in their backyards. Regardless of whether you live in an urban or suburban area or in the country, put out bird feed and you'll attract birds and, guaranteed, you'll attract squirrels as well. Since many

Once squirrels discover the free handouts available from bird feeders, they can become major problems.

Squirrels often destroy feeders to get to the feed.

squirrels are fairly social, once one squirrel finds the food source, others in the community quickly learn about it as well. A number of squirrels regularly visiting a feeder can quickly become a major nuisance and not only keep birds from using the feeder, but also quickly run up a hefty feed bill. Squirrels can also literally destroy a bird feeder in their attempts to get at the feed. Some folks don't mind squirrels at their feeders, though. We have one very fat fox squirrel that regularly visits one of ours. But if you would prefer to keep nuisance squirrels away from your bird feeders, it can be done in several ways.

Discouragement Tactics

The first step is to deny squirrels access to the bird feeder. That, however, is fairly hard to do with the ingenious strategies and acrobatic skills squirrels use to get to them. One method is to place them out in the open, away from trees. With their powerful hind legs, squirrels can jump over six feet straight up. And, they can jump more than eight feet horizontally from object to object. With a target lower than their jumping off place, they can increase this distance greatly. This means the feeder must be positioned higher than six feet from the ground and ten to twelve feet from the nearest overhead object.

Many birds, however, will not frequent feeders placed in the open, preferring those positioned near trees or bushes. The birds can perch in or on these havens, observe the feeder, swoop down, grab some feed, and either go back to their safe perch to consume the feed, or have an escape perch should danger threaten.

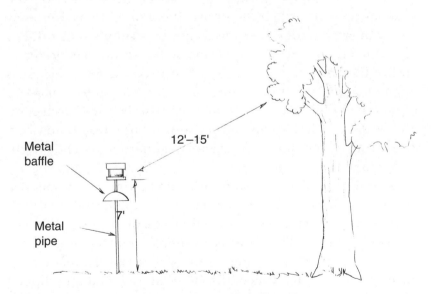

Metal
baffle

12'–15'

Metal
pipe

7'

Most birds prefer feeders with nearby cover, but this invites squirrels. Feeder location and using discouragement tactics can solve some problems.

The support used for the bird feeder can provide some discouragement. Squirrels can descend or ascend just about anything they can get their claws into or around. If you have a high enough tree limb, one method is to suspend the feeder from it. For a couple of years I used a thin piece of rope for this method, and squirrels didn't seem to bother it at first. Unfortunately, they eventually discovered how easy the rope was to climb both down and up, and that was the end of that idea. The next step was to place a length of PVC pipe over the rope. This worked to some extent. But, as the pipe aged and roughened, the squirrels soon learned to climb it as well. The next step was to oil the pipe with lightweight motor oil. It didn't take much, but it did prevent the squirrels from gripping the pipe. One of the best methods with the rope suspension is to place a wide, cone-shaped, angled, sheet metal baffle on the suspension rope. When the squirrels get on it, there is no way they can crawl under it, and as it tips, they simply slide off. For the ultimate in vertical suspension systems, you may prefer to utilize both a pipe and a baffle. Just make sure the feeder is high enough so that the squirrels can't jump up to it and you should be in business. A thin wire can also be used to suspend the feeder and it does discourage squirrel use. Don't, however, use string—they quickly learn to negotiate it or chew right through it.

If you don't have a handy tree limb, you can suspend a feeder on a horizontal wire between two upright supports, such as tree trunks. Again, baffles on either side of the feeder can discourage squirrels. These can be as simple as metal pie pans fastened to a piece of pipe slid over the wire. Discarded plastic soft drink bottles can be drilled with holes in each end and slipped over the wire as well. The holes should be large enough to allow the bottles to spin freely when the squirrel steps on them.

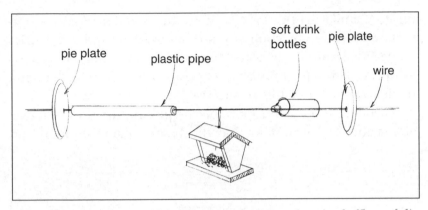

A feeder can also be fastened on a horizontal wire, again using baffles and discouragement tactics to prevent access to the feeder.

Often feeders are placed on poles or posts set in the ground; however, this is not a deterrent. Squirrels quickly learn to climb up the poles, and even negotiate around the wooden platforms at the bottoms of some feeders. The answer again is to use a metal baffle. For stubborn squirrels, two metal baffles may be needed. One tactic is to set a pole, place a cross brace on the pole, and then suspend one, two, or more feeders from the cross brace. The pole must have a baffle on it and the cross braces and feeders must be located far enough from the ground and lower portion of the pole so that the squirrel can't jump up on the post, and then to the feeder. Metal pipes may also be used as the support pole, and they do provide a somewhat slicker surface with less traction for squirrel claws. A variety of baffles are available from several companies. Erva has slide-on baffles that fit poles up to one and five-eighths inches in diameter. These fit on all square, wrought iron, and many tubular poles. Slide the circular collar onto the pole at least four feet up from the ground, tighten the screws until it is firmly attached, and place the baffle on it. A similar baffle is available for any standard four-by-four-inch wood post. The company also has wrap-around disk baffles made of galvanized sheet steel to fit four-by-four-inch wood posts as well as baffles for tubular steel posts. Disk baffles for hanging feeders are also available from Erva.

Feeders can be made portable by placing them on a move-able stand. It's important that the base be large enough and

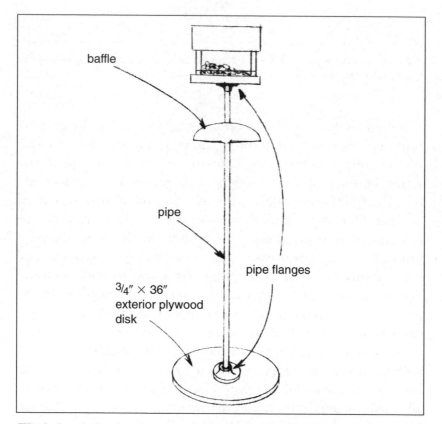

baffle

pipe

pipe flanges

3/4″ × 36″
exterior plywood
disk

The feeder can be placed on a moveable stand consisting of a steel pipe with a baffle.

heavy enough to prevent the wind from blowing the feeder over. Shown is a portable stand I've created for several of our feeders. The stand consists of a wooden base, a pipe flange, a section of galvanized metal pipe, and another pipe flange on top. The feeder is fastened to the top flange.

The Electrifying Situation

A small electric fence charger and a bit of wire can be used to discourage squirrels from getting into post-mounted feeders. We live on a working farm managed for cattle. Electric fence chargers are a way of life with us, not only to contain cattle where we want them, but also to keep unwanted critters away from where we don't want them. We have one charger that is capable of electrifying 100 miles of fencing. Contrary to popular notion, electric fence chargers do not electrocute or injure small animals. These chargers, however, definitely get their attention. To test my hotter chargers, I simply hold a LONG piece of grass to the fence. I start at the tip and move the grass stem up until I keep getting hotter and hotter charges and the jolt becomes extremely uncomfortable. Regardless of the critter, they quickly learn to avoid the shock. But, as I've learned the hard way, they also quickly learn when the fence is not on.

It doesn't take a large charger to hot-wire a bird feeder support post, and it only takes a few feet of wire. Small, battery-operated chargers are more than sufficient for the chore. Any electric fence transmitting wire will do. We use a product called "polywire" for portable fencing on the farm. Polywire consists of several strands of plastic interwoven with tiny strands of metal. It will easily shape around anything and is cut with a sharp knife to the length needed. It's important to remember how electricity conducts its "shock." The wire must be grounded by driving a metal stake into the ground and connecting the stake with a wire to the ground connection on the charger.

Squirrel-Resistant Feeders

In the past there has been no such thing as a squirrel-proof bird feeder. Many newer bird feeders are more squirrel resistant than others and some are almost squirrel-proof. Eventually, however, squirrels will learn how to defeat most "squirrel-proof" feeders.

Do-It-Yourself Feeders

You can easily make a variety of feeders that are squirrel resistant. Many are simple and economical to make from recycled materials. The pop bottle feeder shown has a top cover and enclosed perch too small for squirrels to rest on. Although they can "squirrel" around the top, the opening is fairly small—somewhat of a discouragement. The feeder is easy to make from a discarded plastic soft drink container, a piece of hardware cloth, and a small dowel.

Finch feeders and some other feeders can be made more squirrel resistant by placing cages of hardware cloth around their openings. This allows birds to push their beaks through the openings to the feed, but doesn't allow squirrels to reach their paws through to grasp feed.

House window bird feeders are also more squirrel resistant, primarily due to the closeness of the house and the visibility of people inside.

You can also make an unusual feeder with a hinged, spring-loaded perch. The spring is strong enough that birds can sit on it, but the weight of a squirrel causes the critter to be unceremoniously dumped on the ground. The trick is getting the correct

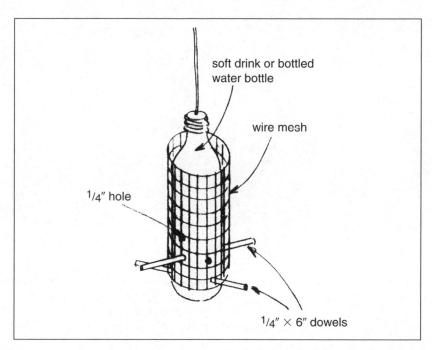

soft drink or bottled
water bottle

wire mesh

1/4" hole

1/4" × 6" dowels

You can easily make a squirrel-resistant finch feeder from a discarded plastic
soft drink or water bottle. Protect the feeder with a hardware cloth guard.

size and tension spring. Construction of the feeder, however, is
fairly easy.

A simple platform bird feeder can be made squirrel resistant
with the addition of a piece of hardware cloth placed over the
feeding surface.

Purchased Feeders

A number of purchased feeders are also available. Make sure
you buy ones with warranties against squirrel damage, since bird

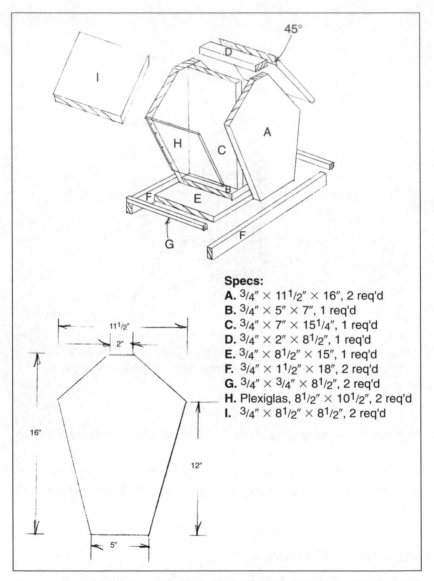

Specs:
A. $3/4'' \times 11^{1}/2'' \times 16''$, 2 req'd
B. $3/4'' \times 5'' \times 7''$, 1 req'd
C. $3/4'' \times 7'' \times 15^{1}/4''$, 1 req'd
D. $3/4'' \times 2'' \times 8^{1}/2''$, 1 req'd
E. $3/4'' \times 8^{1}/2'' \times 15''$, 1 req'd
F. $3/4'' \times 1^{1}/2'' \times 18''$, 2 req'd
G. $3/4'' \times 3/4'' \times 8^{1}/2''$, 2 req'd
H. Plexiglas, $8^{1}/2'' \times 10^{1}/2''$, 2 req'd
I. $3/4'' \times 8^{1}/2'' \times 8^{1}/2''$, 2 req'd

You can also build your own bird feeders fairly easily. The feeder shown isn't squirrel proof, but can be protected with barriers.

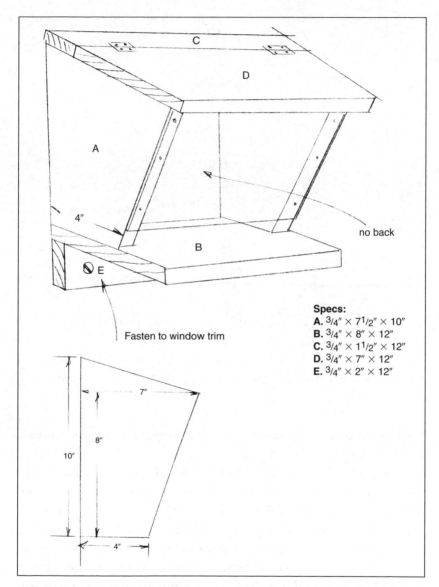

Specs:
A. $3/4'' \times 7^1/2'' \times 10''$
B. $3/4'' \times 8'' \times 12''$
C. $3/4'' \times 1^1/2'' \times 12''$
D. $3/4'' \times 7'' \times 12''$
E. $3/4'' \times 2'' \times 12''$

Fasten to window trim

no back

A house window feeder can easily be made to allow you to observe the birds at close range.

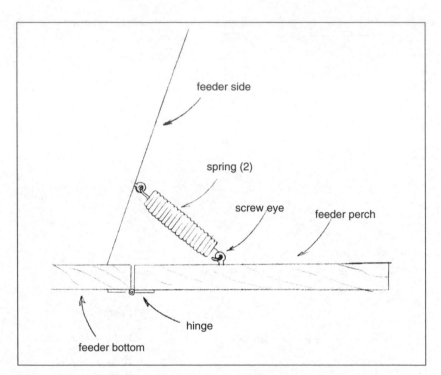

You can add a hinged perch to your homemade feeder that drops the squirrel off.

feeders have been known to take a beating from these critters—even the best of bird feeders.

Many bird feeders are handcrafted of wood in local shops and sold through local stores. Most of these are more "aesthetic" and can add color and style to a backyard. They are rarely pest proof, although the means of mounting them as mentioned can add squirrel resistance to any feeder. Most decorative feeders are table or post mounted. Prices range from a few dollars to several hundred, depending on the craftsmanship and elaborateness of the construction. Metal bird feeders are

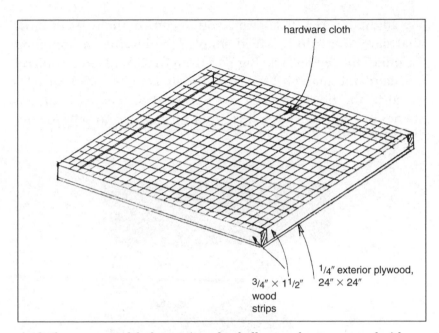

A platform or ground feeder consists of a shallow wooden pan covered with hardware cloth. It allows birds access but keeps squirrels away from the feed.

also available, although there are fewer of them due to their greater cost. The Triple-Bin from Homestead is available from Wal-Mart, Orscheln, Ace Hardware, Lowe's, and Home Depot. The Triple-Bin bird feeder is an extremely durable steel construction that features three separate compartments with acrylic sides for easy viewing of how much feed is available. It also has steel perches and an easily removable steel top for filling. With the triple-bin design you can offer several varieties of feed, all in one feeder.

Domed bird feeders, utilizing a clear or colored plastic dome over the feeder tray, are excellent choices in areas with inclement weather and are also somewhat squirrel resistant. Many are adjustable as well, allowing you to control the types of birds that have access to the feed simply by adjusting the opening height of the feeder. The Big Top from Droll Yankees is squirrel resistant and small bird selective. By adjusting the seed valve located in the bowl, you can use any kind of seed. It is fifteen inches in diameter, has a three-quart capacity, and sells for under $100.

A number of manufactured squirrel-resistant bird feeders are available, including the Ultimate Feeding System from Havahart. (Photos courtesy Havahart)

The Squirrel Proof Bird Feeder from www.bugspray.com features a unique design that provides access to the seed in a bowl-like container with a dome over the top. The top is spring-loaded, and when squirrels climb down from above, the top drops down from their weight and closes over the seed. The top is made from stainless steel, which prevents squirrels from chewing through it. One model has a clear plastic bottom bowl, allowing you to see at a glance how much feed is available; however, squirrels may eventually learn to chew through it. A stainless steel bottom-bowl model is also available, which they can't chew through. These inexpensive feeders sell for around $20.

The Squirrel Free Bird Feeder from Whatever Works Garden & Home Pest Control features two clear-plastic domes, one on top and one on the bottom to hold the seed. When squirrels attempt to get to the bird feed, the lid slides shut, locking the squirrel out. When the squirrel jumps off, the bird feeder springs open with the birdseed protected. Price is about $10.

Tube bird feeders are especially popular as finch feeders. A wide variety are available in either single or multiple tubes. One advantage of tube feeders is you can afford to own many, dispense a variety of seeds, and attract a greater variety of birds to your backyard. Haven bird feeders are primarily hanging, tube-style feeders with a cage constructed around the tube. These are premium feeders that provide smaller birds with sanctuary while they are feeding. Haven bird feeders are excellent choices in neighborhoods where squirrels, cats, and nuisance birds pose threats. Prices range from under $50 to over $150 for the various Haven feeders. Following are some excellent choices in tube-style feeders:

The Duncraft Metal Haven Wild Bird Feeder from Wild Birds Forever is a hanging feeder with six seed ports. Plastic-coated safety wire allows small songbirds to enter, but prevents squirrels and larger birds from feeding. The fencing around the feeder offers perching space for lots of birds. All-metal trays, ports, cap, and base prevent squirrel damage. A fifteen-and-a-half-inch re-cycled polycarbonate plastic tube, seven and a half inches in diam-eter, holds one and a half pounds of sunflower or wild birdseed mix. This is the company's bestseller and its price is less than $50. A ten-and-a-half-inch diameter model is priced slightly higher.

The Ultimate Feeder from Havahart is the first three-tube feeder manufactured. Two sunflower and mixed seed tubes and a thistle tube allow this feeder to dispense nine pounds of three different seeds simultaneously and independently. The feeder comes complete with a squirrel guard and large seed tray. Mount your feeder on the company's ultimate pole and baffle and you can make the installation more squirrel resistant. A number of other tube-style feeders are also available from the company and all come with a dome over the tube. The Hava-hart Infinite Feeding System is an extra large feeder with two in-dependent seed compartments that are separated by a unique flow valve. After being filled with three gallons of seed, this valve is closed and the upper seed reservoir and its eight feeding sta-tions are physically separated from the bottom eight feeding sta-tions. These feeding stations are epoxy-coated die-cast metal. It comes with a clear squirrel guard, pole baffle, and pole and ground sleeve. The Infinite completely disassembles for easy cleaning and is "totally squirrel proof."

Droll Yankees has a number of tube-style feeders, including some with domes for weather protection. Their B-7 Domed Cage feeder has a ten-inch-diameter enclosure and a broad fourteen-and-three-quarters-inch cover to keep rain and snow off the large two-and-a-half-quart capacity feeder. A spring clamp holds the cover firmly in place against the wire cage. The black wire has standard one-and-a-half-inch openings that work well to keep squirrels out, while allowing songbirds easy entrance. The cage comes off in a jiffy for easy cleaning of the feeder. Also available from the company is their Sunflower Domed Cage Feeder. The popular CJM15G feeder is surrounded by an eight-inch-diameter green wire cage that effectively restricts the entrance of gray squirrels while allowing songbirds easy access through the one-and-a-half-inch openings. A more elegant black cage model is also available. The Droll Yankees Thistle Domed Cage Feeder features an eight-inch-diameter wire cage with one-and-a-half-inch squares that restrict squirrels and larger birds, but favors finches and other smaller birds. The company also sells Retro Fit Cages that can be added to an existing tube feeder to create a discriminating feeder and save seed by keeping out squirrels and larger birds. The coated green wire is formed into an eight-inch-diameter enclosure that easily attaches to a number of feeders.

Droll Yankees also has a Squirrel Guard that provides protection from both squirrels and the weather. The polycarbonate dome can be adjusted on the brass rod for use over any hanging feeder. The Squirrel Guard has an eighteen-inch diameter.

One of the more unusual, and most entertaining, bird feeders is the Droll Yankee Flipper. The Yankee Flipper may be the definitive squirrel-proof feeder. Birds love it, but squirrels are prevented from eating from it in a way that will make you smile. The weight-activated feeding perch is calibrated to react to a squirrel's size. When a squirrel steps on the perch, a connection is made with a motor that makes the perch spin, and the squirrel is flipped off the feeder, thus the name "Yankee Flipper." The unit comes with rechargeable NiCad batteries and a battery charger and sells for a little over $100.

Weight-Sensitive Feeders

Bird feeders with weight-sensitive feeding platforms can also be used to discourage squirrels. The Deluxe Squirrel Proof

Feeder from www.bugspray.com has a weight-sensitive ledge that birds must rest on to gain access to the seed. By controlling the setting of two springs located in the back of the house, you can set the ledge to lower when the weight applied is slightly heavier than the average bird. This will prevent squirrels and other animals from gaining access to the seed. This house features a seed-holding bin that will hold a lot of seed; three to five pounds of most seed will fit at one time, which cuts down on the amount of time spent refilling the feeder. The ledge can be set so even the lightest of animals will cause it to close—a great feature if you have rats or flying squirrels feeding at the feeder as well as tree squirrels. The housing is also extremely tough, made of heavy gauge metal that is too strong for larger animals such as raccoons to pull apart, and is priced at a little over $50.

The Squirrel-Resistant Feeder from Lee Valley Tools features a perch as a balance beam attached to a sliding door. The balance can be adjusted so that any desired perch weight causes the door to close the feeder. You can set the weight to accommodate songbirds and to frustrate squirrels and crows. The company notes that although it is effective against black squirrels, immature red squirrels can sometimes infiltrate due to their small size and craftiness. The feeder is an all-metal construction, and holds one and a half gallons of seed. It can be hung or pole mounted and costs around $50.

Havahart sells a variety of bird feeders designed to keep squirrels from feeding. The Metal Squirrel Proof Feeders have Plexiglas windows that enable seed monitoring. Lifting the roof fills the seed reservoir. The bottom of the feeder is pitched to allow seed to flow into the feeding area and the feeder has a barn-siding appearance. The sensitive perch spring allows you to adjust the feeder to prevent squirrels and large birds from feeding. The metal perch closes access to the seed based on

Weight-sensitive bird feeders, such as the Perky-Pet feeder shown, also solve squirrel problems. Any amount of weight on the feeder perch and the food supply is shut off.

your choice of sensitive or firm weight settings. The metal feeder is more sanitary and will not absorb bacteria or mold.

Platform Feeders

Ground-feeding birds such as doves, sparrows, and juncos need a large platform to feed. Due to the nature of their feet, these birds are unable to use many feeders. Feed for these birds shouldn't, however, simply be thrown on the ground, unless the feeding area is changed every day or so. Feeding directly on the ground in the same place can create a health hazard, and during the spring and summer months, seed germination can also be a problem. Platform feeders are easily made and are also available for purchase. They are available in two styles: elevated and ground. The ground style is simply a tray placed on the ground. An elevated style has short legs to keep it just slightly off it. Neither of these, of course, are squirrel proof. You can also position a platform feeder on a tall steel post with a baffle to make it squirrel resistant.

The patented Duncraft Squirrel Blocker Squirrel Proof Platform Feeder, from Wild Birds Forever, has a screen system that lets birds feed but stops the squirrels. The plastic base incorporates drainage holes in the bottom to keep your seed fresh and dry. The platform feeder is easily assembled and simple to clean. A hanging wire is included. Its dimensions are eleven and three-quarters inches wide, fourteen and a half inches long, and one and three-quarters inches tall. The feeder carries a three-year guarantee from the manufacturer.

The Droll Yankee Giant Seed Tray and Squirrel Guard mounts on their Garden Pole and is held in place by a squeeze clamp, which is included. It catches seeds spilled from feeders above and is a great favorite of ground-feeding birds as well. Its broadly curved edge prevents squirrels from getting to your feeders when placed four feet or higher on the pole. This feeder is eighteen and a half inches in diameter and has a one-quart capacity.

Feeders for ground-feeding birds can be filled with inexpensive bulk seed including white proso millet and cracked corn. Platform feeders should be filled with black-oil sunflower seeds or corn.

Other Feeders

Window bird feeders are extremely popular—mainly because they bring the birds virtually right into your home for closer observation. A wide variety of styles are available. Some are fairly economical, made of lightweight acrylic, and attach to the window with suction cups. Others are larger wooden frames made to fit snugly into the frame of your windowsill. The latter allow you to fill the seeder and clean it easily from within your house. Window feeders or feeders placed close to any glass surface can cause birds to fly into the glass and injure themselves. Placing decals on the glass close to the feeder can help prevent any such catastrophes.

Erva carries a full line of squirrel-proof feeders, including: Pagoda Masterpiece at a little under $100; Birdseed Vault at a little under $50; The Squirrel-Selective, Selective Haven, and Peanut Selective Haven for black-oil sunflower seeds or peanuts, all at a little over $50; Absolute II Bird Feeder priced at a bit under $100; and Create-a-Haven at a little over $20.

Bird Watcher's Marketplace also carries the Perky-Pet Squirrel-Be-Gone models priced under $20, Varicraft Bouncer Squirrel Proof Feeder at around $70, Mandarin Sky Café at around $50, Absolute II Squirrel Proof Feeder at around $70, and a number of Droll Yankees feeders already mentioned.

Suet Feeders

Finally, a squirrel-resistant suet feeder is available from Wild Birds Forever. The Duncraft Suet Haven Wild Bird Feeder holds one standard suet cake. The fencing around the feeder offers perching space for lots of birds. A safety-coated plastic cage allows birds safe feeding, but prevents squirrels from sharing in the bounty. The feeder is eight inches high and eight and a half inches in diameter. It carries a lifetime warranty from the manufacturer.

Electronic Feeders

This may be one of the world's most effective and unique squirrel-free bird feeders. When a squirrel lands on WildBill's bird feeder, he receives a harmless static sting. This surprises him and he jumps off. He may return only to be surprised again—but now he's been conditioned to avoid it. The feeder also works on raccoons and other critters. Birds, however, don't feel the sensation. The large seed hopper has a ten-pound capacity with eight ports for feed. A battery charge indicator tells battery power. The feeder has the ASPCA Seal of Approval, is priced at less than $100, and is available from BirdWatchers Wild Bird Products.

Feeding Tips

Providing several feeders in a variety of styles and offering a smorgasbord of feed allows a greater number of birds, as well as a wider variety of them, to be attracted. Following are suggestions from the U.S. Fish & Wildlife Service on food selections for the various types of feeders and the birds they attract.

Tube Bird Feeder with Black-Oil Sunflower Seeds

This type of feeder and feed attracts goldfinches, chickadees, woodpeckers, nuthatches, titmice, redpolls, and pine siskins. By adding a tray to the tube feeder you can also attract cardinals, jays, crossbills, purple finches, white-throated sparrows, house finches, and white-crowned sparrows.

Tray or Platform Feeder with Millet

This feed and feeder attracts doves, house sparrows, blackbirds, juncos, cowbirds, towhees, white-throated sparrows, tree sparrows, white-crowned sparrows, and chipping sparrows.

Tray or Platform Feeder with Corn

This attracts starlings, house sparrows, grackles, jays, juncos, bobwhite quail, doves, ring-necked pheasants, and white-throated sparrows.

Platform Feeder or Tube Feeder and Tray with Peanuts

This attracts cardinals, chickadees, grackles, house finches, titmice, house sparrows, starlings, mourning doves, white-throated sparrows, jays, and juncos.

Niger Thistle Feeder with Tray

This feed and feeder attracts goldfinches, house finches, purple finches, redpolls, pine siskins, doves, chickadees, song sparrows, dark-eyed juncos, and white-throated sparrows.

Hanging Suet Feeder

This feeder attracts woodpeckers, wrens, chickadees, nuthatches, kinglets, thrashers, creepers, cardinals, and starlings.

Hanging Peanut Bird Feeder

Peanuts attract woodpeckers, chickadees, and titmice.

Fruit in Feeders

Fruit attracts orioles, tanagers, mockingbirds, bluebirds, thrashers, cardinals, woodpeckers, jays, starlings, thrushes, cedar waxwings, and yellow-breasted chats.

Probably the best all around feed for the price is a mixture of millet, milo, and sunflower seeds. Sunflower seeds should make up at least 25 percent of the mix. Chicken scratch or cracked corn is one of the most economical feeds, but the mixture tends to attract starlings and house sparrows. Feeding sunflower seeds alone is an excellent choice. Black-oil sunflower seed is the preferred variety. Striped sunflower seed can also be used, but it is not as readily eaten by as many species. If you want to attract goldfinches, you'll need thistle seed, which is a bit more costly. Peanut butter is another favorite, but it can also get expensive. One method of defeating nuisance squirrels is to provide safflower seed instead of sunflower. Squirrels aren't nearly as fond of safflower seeds.

Once you start feeding the birds, don't stop. This is particularly true throughout the winter months when other food sources may not exist.

Keep all bird feeders clean. Songbirds can fall prey to diseases that are easily promoted by dirty feeders and watering devices. In some parts of the country, with wide temperature fluctuations, periods of several days of warm weather during the winter months can bring about mold and diseases such as salmonella. According to Karen Rowe, non-game and endangered wildlife biologist with the Arkansas Game and Fish Commission, "Some individual birds carry the salmonella bacteria in any bird population. Stress, such as cold weather, causes the bacteria to multiply in the intestines. The bacteria are then expelled in the droppings. Crowding at bird feeders then infects other birds. Not all infected birds die, but those who survive can become carriers."

Anyone keeping a bird feeder or bird-watering device should clean the devices regularly. A household bleach solution is the cheapest and best disinfectant. A mixture of one part bleach to ten parts warm water should be used. Rubber gloves should be worn while cleaning the devices.

Any dead birds should be picked up and disposed of as soon as possible to prevent infection to dogs, cats, and any other animals that might prey on the carcass. To pick up the bird without touching it, a plastic sandwich bag can be turned inside out and over the hand like a glove. Pick up the bird and turn the plastic bag back right side out over the bird. Zip the bag shut. Although the chance of infection from touching the bird is very slight, you should always wash your hands vigorously with hot soapy water after cleaning feeders or picking up dead birds.

Bird feeders that force birds to perch while eating also help in keeping the food clean. If the birds are hopping around on a tray of food there is a much greater chance that fecal material will contaminate the food than if the birds are perched on a rail and reaching for the food.

Watering devices are also potential bacteria incubators. A device where the birds can't bathe or perch with their tails over the water can help. Any device should be cleaned and disinfected during the cold months.

According to Rowe there is little information on the effects of salmonella on songbird populations. Because very cold weather and the resultant crowding at feeders are usually only sporadic, the problem often disappears in a few days to a few weeks. Following are some suggestions for safe bird feeding:

1. Avoid crowding at feeders by providing increased feeder space.
2. Keep feeder and surrounding area clean of waste food and droppings.
3. Provide "safe" feeders. Sharp edges or points can scratch birds and invite infection.
4. Throw away any musty, wet, or moldy feed.
5. Disinfect containers or scoops that have been in contact with bad food.
6. Clean and disinfect feeders at least every month, more often if you notice sick birds or in periods of extreme stress. To clean, wear rubber gloves and scrub feeders with warm, soapy water, then immerse in a bleach solution for two to three minutes. Allow to air dry.
7. Make bird feed containers rodent proof because rodent droppings can also contaminate the food.

Protecting Birdhouses

Many people who feed birds also erect birdhouses to attract songbirds. According to the U.S. Fish & Wildlife Service, squirrels and other predators can literally wreck a bird's home. Fox squirrels, and sometimes gray squirrels, can become a very serious menace to birdhouses and to the birds themselves. Once inside the birdhouse, squirrels make a meal of the eggs and young. If you find the entrance hole to your birdhouse enlarged, chances are a fox squirrel is the culprit. Adding a sheet metal predator guard to the hole, so that squirrels can't chew and enlarge it, is one method of solving the problem.

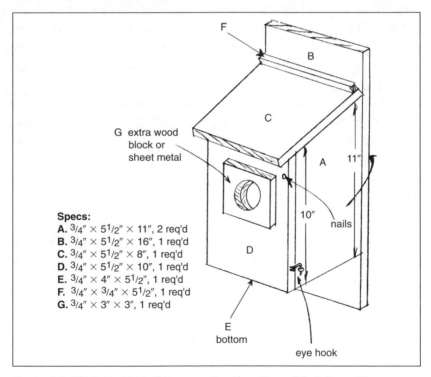

Specs:
A. $3/4'' \times 5^1/2'' \times 11''$, 2 req'd
B. $3/4'' \times 5^1/2'' \times 16''$, 1 req'd
C. $3/4'' \times 5^1/2'' \times 8''$, 1 req'd
D. $3/4'' \times 5^1/2'' \times 10''$, 1 req'd
E. $3/4'' \times 4'' \times 5^1/2''$, 1 req'd
F. $3/4'' \times 3/4'' \times 5^1/2''$, 1 req'd
G. $3/4'' \times 3'' \times 3''$, 1 req'd

Squirrels will also raid birdhouses, eating the eggs and fledglings. Use tree guards and cover the opening with metal or doubled wood to keep squirrels from gnawing the entrance hole wider.

Other Bird House Predators

Cats, dogs, snakes, raccoons, and opossums can also be serious problems. Raccoons and opossums will stick their front paws inside nest boxes and try to pull out the adult, young, and eggs. Again, adding a predator guard to the birdhouse or to its pole support is a simple solution. Nesting birds are also very vulnerable to cats, as are fledglings and birds roosting for the night. Although some people place bell collars on their pets, these offer little protection. Nailing a sheet metal guard or cone to a tree trunk holding nest boxes is unsightly, but it may deter felines. Houses mounted on metal poles are the most difficult for predators to reach, especially if you smear the poles with petroleum jelly and a hot pepper mixture. Snakes are also predators of birds, and can easily worm their way up almost any pole and into the house. Snake-proof your house by putting it on a metal pole slathered with a petroleum jelly and hot red cayenne pepper mix.

Other Solutions

Squirrel repellents can also be used to keep the pests from feeders. A wide variety are available; some work great, others are not quite as effective. Repellents are not, however, as effective as creating the barriers previously mentioned. And, for the most part, repellents need to be regularly replaced. A number of commercial repellents are available. The 4-The-Birds Gel Repellent, from www.bugspray.com, is a clear, gel-like material that is applied where squirrels want to climb, for instance, on feeder poles. It does not dry and will withstand rain and sun. Squirrels will avoid treated surfaces. The gel comes in a tube that fits in caulking guns and each tube will treat ten or more linear feet, depending on the width in which it is applied.

Scoot Squirrel, from Whatever Works, is an all-natural repellent. Scoot Squirrel can be applied to the feeder and will not harm birds. Active ingredients include red pepper and castor oil.

Get Away liquid repellent (Model 5300) from Havahart repels squirrels from the bird feeder. Get Away repels the squirrels by taste and odor, yet it has a pleasant lemon scent that is not offensive to humans. Liquid repellent lasts seven to ten days and should definitely be reapplied after a rain or new growth. Its active ingredients are capsaicin pepper oil and oil of mustard.

One unusual method of repelling squirrels from bird feeders is to use a product called Squirrel Away Bird Food. Squirrel Away is actually a fine powder made of hot peppers that you mix into your regular birdseed. Birds aren't affected because their taste buds don't perceive spiciness. Squirrels, however, don't relish the hotness. The Good Housekeeping Institute tested Squirrel Away.

If you have really serious squirrel problems with your bird feeders and houses, you may wish to consider using Nixalite as a barrier. Nixalite was actually first created to deter pigeons. Nixalite is made of metal strips, two to four feet long, with needle-sharp points protruding from the strips in a 180-degree radius. The strips are about a quarter inch wide and are made of 302 stainless steel. The strips are extremely pliable and can be easily positioned in a variety of ways to protect the top of a feeder, the rope suspending the feeder, or placed on the post holding the feeder. The latter does pose some danger to pets, and especially to young children who may play in the yard. One solution is to place the material higher than the children and pets can reach on the pole. Nixalite is designed to discourage squir-

Nixalite, a metal barrier with needle-sharp points, can also be used to prevent squirrels from getting to feeders. Note the animal barrier on top of the feeder as well. Keep out of reach of pets and children. (Photo courtesy Nixalite)

rels. It is not, however, designed to trap or injure the squirrels. According to the company, Nixalite will not harm squirrels or the birds using the feeder if properly used. Nixalite is also an excellent material to protect pole-mounted birdhouses.

Invite 'Em In

If you can't beat 'em, invite them in. Providing separate feeders for squirrels is one great way of keeping the squirrels from your bird feeders. Simple platforms or shelves attached to trees and kept filled with corn or sunflower seeds will readily attract squirrels. A whole-ear corncob stuck on the sharpened end of a nail driven into the platform will also attract squirrels and keep them occupied longer than loose feed.

Squirrel Antics

Some folks have found squirrel feeders can provide a great show. Any number of feeders can be fashioned to create amusing situations. These include squirrel chairs that seat the little varmints, as well as squirrel tables. One of the more unusual squirrel feeders I've seen is a rotating corncob holder. When the squirrel climbs out on the arm to get at the corn, the arm tips and swings, providing lots of entertainment.

When creating these types of feeders, however, don't make them too complicated. If the squirrels can't easily get at the food, they will soon ignore their feeder and go back to your bird feeders.

Chapter 10 provides more information on attracting and feeding squirrels for those who enjoy watching their antics.

3

Lawns, Gardens, and Flowers

Oh, the damage squirrels can do to lawns, gardens, and flowers—quickly becoming an enemy of any serious gardener. Squirrels eat and they dig; it's as simple as that. With their taste for almost anything edible, squirrels quickly discover the yummy delights found in gardens, flowerbeds, and even container-grown flowers. Flower buds, seeds, bulbs, sweet corn in any stage, tomatoes, young peas, beans, you name it—if you grow it, they will come. What squirrels don't eat they destroy by their digging in search of food. Or, in the case of property with nut trees, squirrels destroy lawns and gardens when burying their hoard of nuts gathered from the neighborhood trees. Nut-burying squirrels have devastated more than one lawn.

For many years, with three kids growing up, and living on a farm with a fairly large yard, we had the solution. We planted four gardens. One was a half acre of sweet corn. One was a quarter acre of potatoes. One was planted with tomatoes, peppers, peas, beans, and other vegetables. The fourth was next to the edge of the woods bordering our yard and planted with a variety of leftover seeds of all types. We called it our "wildlife garden,"

Squirrels can wreak havoc in your lawn, garden, and flowerbeds.

and believe me, all manner of wildlife visited it, including squirrels, rabbits, deer, turkeys, raccoons, opossums, and just about any other animal that walked, flew, or crawled.

When our children left home, we no longer needed to grow as much food and, as we became older, we began to scale back our gardens. We're now down to two: a quarter acre of sweet corn and one main garden. Unfortunately, the wild critters we fed for years continue to think of our place as handout city. Therefore, we created food plots more suited to wildlife, but located farther away from our yard. We have two: one on each side of our yard, located in clearings in the timber several hundred yards away. These food plots include clovers, milo, soybeans, millet, and field corn. Yes, it is a lot of work, but we really enjoy the wildlife and providing for them. These food plots allow us to protect our food gardens from most of their visits.

A number of steps can help protect your lawn and garden from squirrels and other wildlife pests, and many of these will work in any yard. They include using repellents as well as creating barriers.

Animal Repellents

A number of commercial squirrel repellents are available for use in gardens. One natural repellent is blood meal, which also adds organic matter to your garden soil. Another common type of repellent is made from the urine of predators—quite often from fox or bobcat. Trappers Choice Coyote Urine, from www.bugspray.com, can be sprayed on trees, the ground, or directly over spots you know squirrels are walking on or digging in to hide nuts. Be sure to treat the entire area where you know the squirrels are active. This will lead the squirrels to believe they are being stalked and that they might be safer in another location. If using Repellent Guards, place sixteen ounces per guard by every activity site or around areas you need to protect, such as gardens and flowerbeds. Repellent Guards, also from www.bugspray.com, offer a better method of dispersing repellents than simply spraying them on the ground. Two types of Repellent Guards are available. The first is a large, strong, plastic container that can be filled with the liquid or dry repellent. A roof protects the contents from rain and sun, but the vents allow the odor to be released in the designated location. These containers are great for sensitive areas to keep the repellent away from children and pets or if you need to remove the product quickly, say for a backyard party. The holding tank separates easily from the securing stake so you can remove the holding tank without removing the stake. When using Coyote Urine, it's best to use eight ounces per guard, and the guards should be placed ten feet apart.

Due to the nature of the device, you might wish to use the second style. These are actually small capsules that are able to hold about a half an ounce of the urine repellent. The capsules are made of strong plastic and have an attached cap, which can be removed for easy filling. To use, place the capsules straight down in the ground. Make sure they are pushed down far enough so the tops are flush with the soil and place them about a foot apart to get proper coverage. Next, use the included eye-dropper to fill each capsule. Once filled, the capsule should be capped. There are two small holes just below the cap on each side of the capsule that will allow the urine to slowly evaporate and release the odor. The cap will protect the capsule's contents from rain and sun.

Either of these styles may be used in gardens, flowerbeds, walkways, around pools, along fence lines, under decks, under sheds, or under your house. When urine repellent is placed out on the ground, it may last only two to three weeks. When used with either guard, the applications last two to three times as long. Most important, the placements will slowly dissipate instead of being washed away, which can happen when urine is placed out without protection and a heavy rain falls.

Another squirrel repellent is Rid-A-Critter Squirrel Repellent. Rid-A-Critter is made of time-release capsules that will last outside for up to two months. Inside, Rid-A-Critter will last as long as three months.

Some solutions contain mothball ingredients mixed with repellent hair materials. One commercial spray is nicotine sulfate. Others, such as Squirrel Away, contain capsaicin oil from hot peppers.

Sprinkling cayenne or ground red pepper on specific plants can deter squirrels. You can also create your own hot pepper spray, but it requires fresh peppers, a blender, rubber gloves, and eye protection. Blend the peppers into a fine powder, mix with water, and spray the solution on your plants. You can also mix the powder with a light oil such as dormant oil tree spray. This tends to stay on the plant longer than the water spray. Remember, though, capsaicin oil is extremely irritating. Do not allow the oil to touch your skin, do not breathe it, and, especially, do not get it in your eyes.

Scoot Squirrel, from Whatever Works Garden & Home Pest Control, is an all-natural solution to the gardener's nuisance squirrels. Scoot Squirrel keeps squirrels away from plants without harming either the plants or the squirrels. Its active ingredients include red pepper and castor oil. You can even spray bulbs with Scoot Squirrel to protect them before planting. Also from the company is Get Away, which keeps raccoons and squirrels away from gardens and lawns as well as out of the garbage. Get Away is a vegetable oil–based product that doesn't pose any harm to friendly birds and animals. For outdoor use, Get Away resists washing away by rain. You can also try EPA-registered Squirrel Chase pouches, which are filled with an all-natural ingredient that leaves a scent squirrels won't go near. Just hang Squirrel Chase pouches in trees, shrubs, or near gardens you want to protect.

The Havahart Liquid Squirrel Repellent discourages digging in landscaped areas. This product repels squirrels by both taste and odor, but it has a pleasant lemon scent that is not offensive to humans.

Homebrew repellents include using household ammonia around plants. Or simply drop mothballs around plants. If you have only a few special plants to protect, another homebrew is a solution of one teaspoon of Lysol or three ounces of Epsom salts added to one gallon of water. These sprays must be repeated frequently since new growth and rain reduce their effectiveness.

One of the most unusual methods of repelling squirrels is the use of a motion-activated water sprayer. The Spray Away product from Havahart senses the animal's heat and movement. It uses a nine-volt battery for thousands of activations. The device shoots water up to thirty-five feet and protects 1,000 square feet. Spray Away pauses for eight seconds after firing, creating a randomness that prevents the animal from becoming accustomed to the repellent. A motion-activated sprinkler from Lee Valley Tools Ltd., operates twenty-four hours a day. The unit uses only two to three cups of water per event, so it can often be used even in communities engaged in water rationing. The smart circuitry automatically dampens sensitivity in windy conditions to prevent false triggering. An adjustable sensitivity control changes the distance the unit can "see." Optional scarecrow decals are included. The unit measures twenty-four inches tall and is ideal for keeping night "visitors," including deer, out of your gardens.

Creating Animal Barriers

Squirrels are basically opportunists. If they find an easy meal, they'll go for it. If you make it too hard to get to the meal, they'll look elsewhere. In gardens or flowerbeds, a more permanent solution is simply to create barriers to prevent squirrels from getting to them. This can only be done, however, in open areas where squirrels can't jump from trees, overhead buildings, or power lines.

Creating cages of hardware cloth can protect individual plants. This is a method we use in our test plots. For several years, we have been testing clovers for deer food plots, but the wildlife will eat the clover regularly, making it hard to deter-

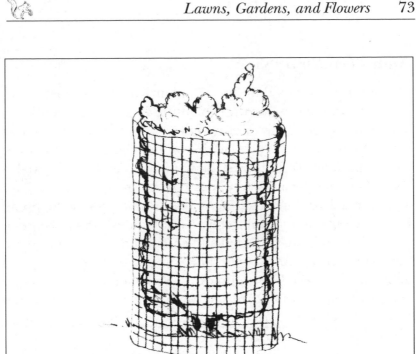

Hardware cloth cages can be used for individual plants.

mine their growth habits. These cages, made with one-quarter-inch hardware cloth, keep a small portion of the plot protected. Simply cut the cloth into a rectangle the size needed to create a round cage to fit over a plant. The ends can be wired together, or use "hog-rings" to fasten them. Adding a top to the cage can discourage persistent squirrels, as well as pesky birds and rabbits. The cages, however, won't prevent damage from burrowing squirrels. To protect plants from them, you will have to extend the wire at least twelve inches below the soil surface. The top must also be kept loose so it can be removed as needed.

Raised Garden Beds

One solution we found for specific plants, and also a method of growing more in less space, is planting in raised garden beds. This is an excellent way of growing plants such as lettuce or carrots, which are relished by squirrels, rabbits, and many other wild creatures. We build the beds of pressure-treated two-by-sixes. They can be any length desired, but make sure you have an easy reach to the center of the bed from each side. Stepping in a raised bed to reach the center would defeat the purpose of it. You don't want to walk on it and compact the soil. A low hardware cloth cage with a removable top protects the plants, yet allows for easy weeding and picking. Another advantage, especially with early-season plants, is that you can use the cage as a form to cover with a piece of clear plastic to protect the tender young plants on cold nights.

The Fenced Garden

You can also fence off an entire garden or flowerbed area. This chore, however, is greater, and again, it's important that squirrels do not have overhead access of any kind. They'll jump into an area such as this quicker than a kid into the old swimming hole.

The garden fence can be decorative, but remember squirrels can climb just about anything. If you need a privacy fence as well, you may consider constructing the fence of wood. In that case, Nixalite can be added around the top edge to deter squirrels from climbing over it.

A hardware cloth fence can also be used to enclose an entire garden area. This will keep out rabbits and squirrels for a while— until they learn how easy it is to climb. This will also not keep out ground-burrowing critters. You will need to create an L-shaped

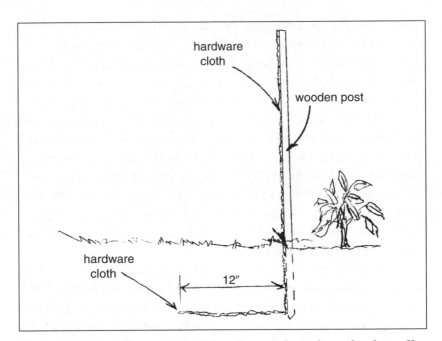

Hardware cloth, with a section buried underground, can be used to fence off a small garden.

underground barrier with the L facing outward to block ground burrowers. To do this, dig a trench about six inches deep and six inches wide in the location of the fence. Position the fence in place and cover the bottom with soil. Remember to provide a "gated" area to get tillers into the garden. The fence should be fairly low, about two feet high, so you can easily step over it.

Electric Fencing

We've always had problems with squirrels and other critters, especially raccoons, with the annual sweet corn patches we raise. These varmints know exactly when the corn is ready to pick, and I understand how and why. With a large sweet corn patch, the smell of ripening corn is an enticement that can be detected a long distance away. Squirrels hit the patch just before dark and at daylight, and the raccoons do night duty. Several years ago, just before the corn was to ripen, a neighbor, an old-time farmer, suggested I string an extension cord into the corn patch and hang a light. I did. The next morning, guess what— the patch had been hit hard. The neighbor then suggested I add a radio, tuned to a rock station, of course, because the loud music would scare off all critters. I did. The next morning my entire patch was decimated. All I did was provide the lights and entertainment for a great party.

Then the lightbulb in my head went off and that's when I discovered electricity. We now raise a full crop of corn—when I don't forget to turn on the electricity. My forgetfulness one year even allowed our cows a full night in the patch. Believe me, they outdid the squirrels and other wild critters in their feasting.

We have a very sophisticated electrical system for our garden, based on our farm experiences. We raise beef cattle and were one of the first in our community to utilize extensive grazing. With this method the cattle are kept in small paddocks fenced off with electric fencing. The cattle are moved every few days, utilizing the forage to the greatest extent. The key to this operation is highly portable electric fencing materials. These materials consist of plastic fencing poles that can easily be pushed or hammered into the ground, plus polywire, a fencing wire made of plastic strands interwoven with tiny metal strands. The wire comes on spools, is easily cut with a knife, and can be tied together in the configurations needed to create a fenced area. The newer electric chargers available these days, such as Kencove low impedance models, are also less dangerous and

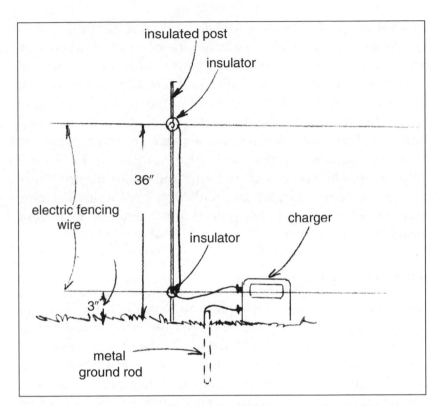

One of the simplest methods of squirrel control is to use an electric fence.

less of a fire hazard than older models. The charge from the fence will kill plants contacting it, but will not create a fire hazard. The shock will not harm animals that touch it, but they definitely get the message.

We use a double wire system for the garden, and it takes about an hour to put up the system on our large corn patch. First, the plastic poles are placed at the corners and down the sides, spacing them about twenty-five feet apart. A wire is run around the poles, fastening to fencing clips about three inches off the ground. This deters squirrels, raccoons, and other small mammals. At the starting pole the wire is run up to a second strand positioned about two and a half feet off the ground. This keeps out the deer. It is important to keep the weeds down under the low fence, a chore that is easy with a power string trimmer. The reason is the weeds act as a ground and can cut down on the power of the shock. Also, visibility of the fence is important. The fence is then connected to an electric fence charger. Electric chargers are available as AC units that plug into household current, DC units that are powered by battery, or solar-powered units.

Deterring the Diggers

Tree squirrels, as well as ground squirrels, dig for a variety of reasons, and the most common reason is to locate foods. Some of their favorite foods include bulbs of flowers such as crocuses and hyacinths, as well as the corms of plants. They also like to chew on the rhizomes of other perennials. The mere fact that perennials are permanently left in the ground permanently makes them more susceptible to the diggers. And once they find a bed of succulent bulbs, the squirrels won't quit until all are consumed. A simple solution to prevent tree squirrels from raiding some of these permanent flowerbeds is to place a wire mesh over them. This works for beds of early spring flowers such as crocuses and also works for the later-flowering tulips. The mesh should be large enough to allow the flowers to sprout through, but small enough so that squirrels can't dig through. Three-quarter or one-inch hardware cloth can be used, as can welded wire mesh commonly used for reinforcing concrete slabs.

Hardware cloth placed over spring flowerbeds can also prevent squirrels from digging up and eating bulbs.

Scare Tactics

Scaring the @#&%* out of squirrels works to a certain extent and for a short period of time. Eventually, however, they learn that scare tactics are just that, tactics, and become immune to them. Yet, sudden noises and movements will at least keep them more wary. Many scare tools are available at garden supply stores. Brightly colored balloons filled with helium and tied just over plants can deter squirrels and birds, especially on days with any wind. Special bright-yellow balloons called "Big-Eye" balloons are made just for this tactic. It's important to move the balloons around daily so the squirrels don't get used to their location. Simply tie the balloons to bricks and move the bricks and balloons as needed.

The great horned owl is one of the squirrel's worst nightmares, and a number of owl "scarecrows" are available. Some even have heads that bob and sway to provide more realism. Place these on a perch above an area and you'll keep the squirrels away. Unfortunately, you'll probably keep the birds away as well. Like other scare tactics, you will probably have to move the perch around from day to day to prevent the squirrels from getting used to having their nemesis around. There are even gator head scare objects, as well as a battery-powered rattlesnake that has a motion head and tail. In snake country it will probably keep squirrels out of your garden, raccoons out of the pet feed, and your neighbor's kids or your least favorite aunt out of about anything as well.

Feeding the Squirrels

Sometimes you just have to share your bounty. We raise bushels of tomatoes and discovered many years ago the best way to keep plants producing is to pick the tomatoes as soon as they show color. This often means picking ten gallons of tomatoes during the height of the season. The tomatoes are then spread out on a flat surface in the shade for several days to a week to continue ripening. We have a seating bench built around a huge oak in our backyard, and one summer I began placing the overflow of ripening tomatoes on the bench. One morning I discovered tomatoes with the ends nibbled. After observing the tomato pile for a while, we saw a chipmunk living in the base of the tree scamper up the trunk onto the back support of the seat, climb down over onto the seat, and feast on a tomato. Actually, the solution for the problem was quite simple: We placed tomatoes with spots or other imperfections on the top of the seat back ledge, within easy reach of the chipmunk. As long as there were tomatoes at this easily reached location, it left the other tomatoes alone. We both shared a bounty of tomatoes all summer.

Other Outside Problems

Squirrels need water, and they will often go to extremes to get to it. Several times I've had to fish dead squirrels out of cattle watering tanks, especially those next to a fence that allows the squirrels easy access. Squirrels can't, however, climb back out of the tank if they fall in. The easiest solution is to move the tank away from the fence. But sometimes that makes it difficult to fill the tank with a garden hose. I eventually constructed a steel ramp that rests against one side of the tank. It is welded of light-gauge, perforated steel mesh, and although it rusts through in a couple of years, it's cheap and easy to make. The mesh provides plenty of footing for squirrels to climb in and out of the tank. Squirrels, as well as other critters, including armadillos, are also prone to fall into swimming pools. If they don't have an escape ramp out, they drown. One solution is to keep water available for squirrels, birds, and other critters. Birdbath waterers offer some water, but a ground-based watering pool offers more water for more creatures. Birdbaths and ground-based watering pools can prevent many accidents for wildlife searching for water in your backyard.

Ultrasonic Devices

Ultrasonic devices emit a noisy, intense ultrasonic sound which is based on "psychoacoustic jamming" principles. These sounds do everything from disrupting the animal's nervous system to being perceived as a loud, continuous jackhammer pounding. Some of these sounds may be detectable by people and are in the frequency range clearly heard by rodents. The Ultra Sound Repeller emits a high sound that is in the animal's sound stress range. The Ultra Sound Repeller comes in two designs, running on either four C-cell batteries or a unit that can run off batteries or an AC adapter that plugs into an electrical outlet. Both feature a "volume" knob that you can adjust for the target animal. A motion detector is also built into the units. These units are placed in outside areas you want to keep squirrels away from, including decks, pools, grass, and any other spot roaming activity is not wanted. The devices project the high-frequency sound up to eighty feet, although they're most effective at around fifty. Each unit is able to cover up to 180 degrees of space and an area of up to 3,000 square feet. The key is positioning the unit so that it has an unobstructed projection of the sound it emits. Shrubs, trees, bushes, and any vegetation will take away from this coverage by muffling the sound waves. For best results, try to mount the device high enough to get the signal up over any objects that might absorb the signal. You also need to keep the unit angled correctly, however, so that the sound will be at ground level or treetop, depending on where you want to stop the squirrel activity. The AC/battery unit is around $100, while the battery-operated unit costs much less.

The Ultrasonic Squirrel Deterrent from Whatever Works covers a smaller, fourteen-by-fifty-six-foot area, is weather resistant, and comes with an AC adapter and twelve-foot cord for about half the price of the larger Ultra Sound unit.

Just a Big Dog

Of course, one of the best tactics for keeping squirrels out of your backyard garden and lawn is a dog. My Irish setter does a

Sometimes the only squirrel repellent you need is a big dog.

good job of chasing squirrels from our yard. But dogs don't have to be big. One of the best squirrel repellents I can remember was a little rat terrier named Gidget. Although she wasn't much bigger than a big fox squirrel, she was deadly to them. She also kept the rat population in Dad's barn to a minimum. When I was a kid we used to feed our animals sheaf oats. The oats were cut with the seeds in place, tied in bundles, and stacked in the barn. At the end of the winter when we were down to the last layer of oats, the fun would begin. We would carefully lift a sheaf with a pitchfork, with Gidget standing at attention. Inevitably, a rat or several mice would scurry from under the oats and the race was on. The feisty little dog even killed a badger one night. Although badgers were several times her size and well known for their ferocity, she won the battle with this one. Dad witnessed the last of the fight with his flashlight after being woken up by the ruckus, and he enjoyed telling the tale of her conquest for many years afterward.

Dogs can, however, be just about as bad for lawns and gardens as squirrels—especially those with landscaped flowerbeds. We've never had a dog yet that could resist digging up and snoozing in the soft, well-kept, cool soil of our flowerbeds. Sometimes it's a trade-off as to which animal is the worst nuisance.

Controlling Groundhogs

Using gas cartridges that produce a fumigating gas when burned can eliminate nuisance groundhogs. These cartridges should only be used in dens located away from buildings because sparks may be thrown. They should also not be used near combustible materials, which include dry grasses and weeds during droughts or dry seasons. You might accidentally start an uncontrollable fire. The cartridges are available at farm and garden supply stores and they produce a carbon monoxide gas, which accumulates in lethal amounts when confined within the groundhog den and burrow system. Carbon monoxide is a humane fumigating gas. The gas cartridges are filled with combustible materials and must be ignited by lighting a fuse on the end of the cartridge. These cartridges are not bombs, and will not explode if properly prepared and used. You should not, however, breathe the smoke.

To use, cut a clump of sod slightly larger than the burrow opening with a spade. Place the sod near it. Next, punch five pencil-size holes in the end-cap of the cartridge. Insert the fuse to half its length into one of the holes. The cartridge is now ready to use. Kneel near the burrow opening, light the fuse, and immediately place the cartridge as far down in the hole as you can reach. Do not throw the cartridge.

Immediately close off the burrow opening by placing the sod, grass side down, over the opening to make a tight seal. Placing the sod grass side down prevents loose dirt from smothering the cartridge. Garbage can covers, sand bags, or other suitable covers can also be used to close off the opening.

Stand by for three or four minutes and watch nearby holes. Plug any holes from which smoke escapes. Repeat until all burrows are closed.

4

Squirrels in the Orchard

If you think the squirrel clan is hard on your lawn, garden, and flowers, wait until they get to your fruit and nut trees. About the only thing squirrels love more than nuts is fresh fruit. And it doesn't have to be totally ripe. Green apples don't seem to bother squirrels nearly as much as little boys, as I discovered early in life.

For the most part, the mast squirrels eat from backyard oak trees is not missed, although they will dig in the yard to bury the nuts for the winter months. They also don't seriously damage oak and hickory nut trees, except to enlarge cavity openings created by woodpeckers. They do eat the buds and catkins of many types of trees, which can hinder mast production. Pecan trees, on the other hand, due to their high oil content, are greatly relished by squirrels from the moment the buds sprout until the last husks open and the pecans fall to the ground. It is estimated a single squirrel can eat ten pounds of the tasty nuts each month of the growing season.

Fruits are another matter. There simply isn't a fruit squirrels don't love. We have a full orchard, with several pear trees, about twenty-five apple trees, a dozen peaches and apricots, as well as

Squirrels love orchards and nut trees as well. They'll eagerly steal your peaches, blueberries, apricots, and pears with the best of them.

cherries. Keeping squirrels out of the trees is a full-time chore. Then there's the blueberry patch nearby. It's fruit compote time for the squirrels when the blueberries begin ripening. I've tried just about everything to deter squirrels from my orchard. In particular, I've had the most trouble with the apricot and pear trees. Both fruits ripen slowly over a period of time, and once the squirrels get on these fruits, it's almost impossible to deter them. My neighbor with the raccoon wisdom suggested that the main reason squirrels target these juicy fruits is a lack of drinking water. He suggested placing pans of water in my orchard. It worked to some degree. At least the squirrels had a beverage to wash down my pears.

An owl scarecrow can protect individual trees, but should be moved daily.

Other methods, in particular the scare tactics, work fairly well in keeping squirrels out of orchards. That is, until they become educated to the fact that the tactics are just that—for scaring.

An owl scarecrow can be effective for protecting individual or a handful of trees. I've also placed pebbles in used aluminum drink cans and tied them to tree branches. The breeze rattles the cans and the pebbles clatter inside. This succeeded for about a week. Commercial scare items, such as the Squirrel Chaser, which has a combination of mothballs and predator hair, are available in a bag that can be hung in the tree. Scare-eye balloons can also work for a period of time. Many of the commercial and homebrew repellents will work on the trunks of isolated trees, until rain washes them away. The predator urine–type repellents are effective on tree trunks.

Ultrasonic repellers, working off electricity, can also deter squirrels. You will, however, need the larger, commercial variety to do much good in an orchard.

Squirrel Barriers

Creating a barrier to the tree is the most effective nonlethal method of minimizing squirrel damage in your orchard. Squirrels can be kept from isolated fruit or nut trees by putting wide bands (three feet) of sheet metal around the trunks. This works if there are no low branches or nearby trees to allow access. It's best to fasten the band with wire through holes punched in the ends of the metal. The band should be removed at the end of the fruit or nut-producing season. If left in place, the band can hamper the growth of the tree and create a mold and disease barrier. If individual trees are near overhead objects, such as power lines, other trees, tall shrubs, or buildings, you will have to add another barrier. Anti-bird nets placed over the trees to

Keeping dead limbs trimmed back and openings filled with mortar will prevent nesting cavities from forming in ornamental trees and backyard orchards.

prevent birds from pecking and eating the fruit will also create a barrier to some degree to squirrels from above—that is, if the metal barrier is also in place around the tree trunk. Unfortunately, these lightweight mesh nets are no matches for the teeth of a determined squirrel.

Woodlot Management

Squirrels love old trees with holes for dens. One way of helping prevent squirrel problems in your backyard orchard, or with nut or ornamental trees, is to keep dead snags and limbs cut away so they don't rot off and produce holes that will attract woodpeckers that peck out the cavities that squirrels love. Small holes should be filled with a mortar mix to discourage woodpeckers and squirrels.

5

Squirrels in Houses, Barns, and Outbuildings

Squirrels, chipmunks, ground squirrels, and especially groundhogs can extensively damage buildings. They chew exterior holes that provide them access to attics and other areas, where they may also gnaw on electrical wiring, creating safety hazards. The full-scale burrowing groundhogs are capable of undermining building foundations. These critters can also bring other pests and diseases into a home. And, more than one person has wondered at the strange noises emanating from the attic in the deepest of night. It's probably not ghosts or demons with big fangs and clawed hands, but the scampering of little clawed feet. Nighttime noises are usually the work of nocturnal flying squirrels, but they're extremely hard to positively identify because they hide extremely well. Flying squirrels tend to burrow down into the insulation, or creep into cracks and crevices, especially when you inspect the attic with a flashlight or switch on the attic light. On the other hand, tree squirrels usually make more noise during the day. When you confront them in the attic, they'll quite often stand their ground. You should also inspect your attic for nests. If you locate a nest, use latex gloves and a stick to determine if there are any young in the nest. If not, you

If things go bump-in-the-night in your attic, it's time to inspect for squirrel "squatters."

may be able to scare the squirrel out of the attic. Once you think you've sealed off the squirrel, locate any openings where it might have come in and—you hope—out, and seal them off. The next day listen very carefully to determine if you have sealed any other squirrels inside. If a squirrel seems desperate to get back in, it may still have young in the attic.

Tree Work

With tree squirrels, one of the first steps is to remove their travelways where possible. Some of the most common travelways are tree branches that overhang the house, and especially those branches that droop down close to the roof. Overhanging branches within eight feet of the roofline should be trimmed

Overhanging branches provide a squirrel highway into your house. Keep over-hanging branches trimmed back, away from your house.

back. This also prevents problems from limbs falling on the house during wind or ice storms and helps prevent the unsightly mildew caused by deep shade as well. Tall shrubs next to the house should also be trimmed back. Once the squirrels get into the shrubs, they can often jump or climb wooden siding to get access to the house. Squirrels can also easily climb brick or stonework.

Utility lines are other very important squirrel pathways, as anyone who has watched them tightrope-walk these lines can attest. The same types of baffles used to prevent squirrels from getting to feeders can be used on overhead telephone lines. These include pie plate–type baffles as well as plastic pipes. It's important not to put too much weight on the line, and also to install the baffles where the wind can't catch them and create other hazards, such

Utility lines also provide access. For squirrel problems with electrical power lines, contact your local power company for advice.

as pulling the lines down. Plastic pipe baffles consist of a four-foot section of PVC pipe. Cut a slit the length of the pipe with a hand-saw. Then spread the pipe using a large screwdriver and slip it over the line. Squeeze the pipe back together once it is installed over the line. Not only does the slick surface of the pipe provide fewer footholds, but also the pipe tends to turn with the weight of the squirrel, throwing it off. You can coat the pipe with a slippery substance, such as petroleum jelly, as a further deterrent. Electric power utility lines are also extremely common squirrel travelways. These lines are, however, dangerous to mess with. If you have problems with squirrels using these lines for access to your house, contact the local utility company for advice.

Flues and chimneys provide access to squirrels, as well as bats and chimney swallows. A chimney cap solves the problem.

Squirrels also frequently venture down flues and chimneys. The installation of a chimney cap will not only keep out squirrels but also bats and swallows as well. All of these critters may use the chimney or flue during the off-season. Chimney caps to fit most flues and chimneys are found at most hardware and home improvement stores and are relatively easy to install. One problem occurs when a squirrel accidentally drops down inside a chimney with a metal liner. If the damper is open, it may end up in your house. One summer we also had a snake enter our house in this manner. If the damper is closed, in some instances the squirrel may not be able to climb back out. In this case, attach a thick rope to the top of the chimney or flue and lower it down to the damper shelf. In time, the squirrel will probably climb up the rope and back out.

House Work

Squirrels can get into your house through the tiniest of holes. The first step is to make a thorough examination of the house exterior, checking for any gnawed holes or rotted areas. A good pair of binoculars can be valuable for this task. If possible, get up on the roof and examine it carefully. The roof can, however, be extremely dangerous. Do not wear slippery shoes, and do not go up on the roof when it is wet with dew, snow, or rain. Some roofs with extremely sharp pitches are not safe to climb on without special equipment. When getting onto the roof, make

Loose or missing shingles and openings around vent pipes and chimneys also provide access.

sure the ladder is safely positioned. Loose or missing shingles or holes in shingles are fairly easy to spot. In fact, water damage in your home may also indicate these types of problems. Other roof areas where problems may exist include the flashing around vent pipes, dormers, chimneys, roof vents, or fans. Examine roof vents very carefully because they are common places for squirrels to enter. It doesn't take as much gnawing to chew through an already existing opening in the vent.

Gutters and downspouts are also common travelways. Tree squirrels can easily traverse up and down the downspouts. Once they reach the gutters, squirrels have a "highway." Install gutter guards and either cover all downspouts with screening or connect them to a buried corrugated pipe. The gutter guards can also prevent squirrels from using the gutters as travelways once

Gutters and downspouts are also squirrel "freeways" to your home. Cover with gutter guards.

they get to the roof from other avenues, such as power lines or overhead tree branches.

Once you've completed your roof examination, it's time to scan the eaves and soffits of the house. Soffits often loosen or rot out from improper shingle application or old shingles that need to be replaced. Once inside the soffits, squirrels have easy access to the attic and other spaces. Carefully check the soffits for any loose areas and rotted or gnawed holes. Quite often there is also a small crack between the fascia board and the roofing material. Squirrels can squeeze through almost any crack. Flying squirrels are especially adept at finding these small cracks and, since their bodies are so flexible, they can squeeze in and out of spots with an ease that would amaze Houdini. Patch all holes with flashing material or one-quarter- or one-

Even the smallest opening in the soffit or fascia boards allows flying squirrels entry. Make sure all openings are closed off, after the squirrels are evicted.

In the case of serious gnawing problems, stuff holes around pipe openings, cracks, or any type of opening with copper wool or Nixalite's STUF-FIT, a soft copper mesh cloth. (Photo courtesy Nixalite)

half-inch hardware cloth. Make sure the patch is extended at least six inches larger than the hole in all directions to prevent the squirrel from gnawing through the patched area. STUF-FIT, from Nixalite, is a great material for patching small holes two inches or smaller. STUF-FIT is a soft copper mesh cloth that can be stuffed into openings to keep out all kinds of unwanted pests. Its unique combination of versatility, strength, and resistance to corrosion makes it the perfect choice for a wide variety of access and exclusion control applications. When compared to STUF-FIT, steel wool and expanding foams, often used for access control, are poor substitutes. The material can be cut to the desired length with scissors and stuffed, pushed, or packed tightly into any small crack, hole, gap, or opening. Make sure STUF-FIT is compacted so it cannot be pulled out or worked loose. The material is available in 100-foot rolls.

In some cases, you may need to replace the soffits with new material. Vinyl soffits to match or contrast with vinyl siding can also be used to cover over entry holes.

Patch any holes in the siding, soffits, and roof edges. Rotted wood should be replaced with new wood. If you spot gnawed entry holes, it is not advisable to shut squirrels out of buildings by simply closing off these openings. First, squirrels may be inside and you can make a bad situation worse if they can't use their normal entry and exit. The squirrels may chew new holes to get out, or they may die inside the building, creating another very serious problem. Even if the squirrels are outside when you fill the holes, squirrels accustomed to using the entrance and attic spaces will simply gnaw holes in other places. Sealing the holes only *after* the squirrels have been removed with repellents is a better method to keep out other squirrels.

Continue your inspection of the structure, inspecting downward. Other prime locations for squirrels, both tree and ground species, include cracks and/or openings in the foundation. Any openings or cracks should be patched with mortar. Check also for buckling siding where the siding overlaps the foundation. Refasten the siding in place. Concrete foundations should extend at least twelve inches above ground level to discourage and prevent the gnawing of holes. Sheet metal, twelve inches high, should be smoothly inserted on all corners above floor or ground level to prevent animals from climbing.

Other prime entry locations include cracks in foundations or loose siding. Fill holes with a mortar patch.

In most instances, a good grade of caulking will suffice for closing openings around pipes.

Air-conditioning pipe openings, and any other openings, no matter how seemingly small, can also be potential entry locations. Stuff copper wool into all these openings and around all entry pipes. Cover all edges of doors and windows subject to gnawing, or where gnawing is evident, with sheet metal or hardware cloth.

Squirrel Repellents

Repellents are useful in keeping squirrels out of buildings and in preventing damage to cedar shingles. One of the better repellents is naphthalene flakes or common mothballs. The flakes are more convenient to use. Four or five pounds of flakes should be scattered liberally about the spaces used by squirrels. Naphthalene is not a permanent repellent since it is necessary to repeat the treatment at short intervals.

To keep squirrels from gnawing on cedar shingles, an effective repellent can be made by adding one pound of copper naphenate to two and a half quarts of mineral spirits, linseed oil, or shingle stain. If the color is not important, two pounds of copper carbonate and three pounds of asphalt emulsion is a good repellent.

A number of commercial repellents for use in buildings are also available. Rid-A-Critter suggests using their Dr. T's repellent in primary marking areas, runs, nests, and feeding areas. Because squirrels learn to solve nesting and feeding problems very quickly, they suggest it is necessary to maintain these barriers for a long period of time, at least two to three months or longer, to gain control. Rid-A-Critter Rabbit and Squirrel Repellent is 100 percent naphthalene. It repels for four months indoors. It drives squirrels from attics, and has guaranteed performance when used as directed. Packaged in a twenty-ounce jar, eight ounces of Rid-A-Critter will treat 200 cubic feet. Ropel Liquid Repellent has a very bitter taste and should be sprayed on areas where squirrels tend to gnaw.

Ultrasonic repellent systems are more effective in repelling squirrels from enclosed spaces of the house. Most units simply plug into a household outlet and the ultrasonic waves repel squirrels, mice, rats, bats, and other critters. Some of the better-quality units have variable settings to target specific pests. Some units emit sonic sounds and electromagnetic waves to add to their repellent capabilities. Humans can't hear the high-frequency sounds, and most units are also harmless to pets, although some pets will probably be able to hear the sounds. Battery-powered units are available for areas without electric outlets.

Although ultrasonic units are effective in repelling new critters, they will rarely drive a squirrel from your attic or other space. These units were originally designed to keep rats and mice from invading warehouses, but they do not kill or drive out critters already using the spaces. First, the squirrel or squirrels must be removed from the area, and live trapping is usually the best choice. Don't use poisons, as the animal will probably die in your home, resulting in a real mess and odor. Once you've removed the animal or animals, then plug all holes as described. Ultrasonic devices can then be used to help prevent entry of new animals. In most instances, you will need more than one unit to cover the average attic, especially an attic with several roof angles and turns. Also, wood and insulation tend to reduce the effectiveness of the sound waves, so make sure the units are installed up and out of any insulation. The better units will also have metal rather than paper speakers. These produce more "volume" and are longer lasting.

Groundhogs can undermine building foundations. Trap the problem animals, fill in the tunnels, and create underground barriers to deter further digging.

Groundhog Damage

Groundhogs love to burrow in the soft dirt of old barns or out-buildings and can undermine and destroy foundations. Although smoke bombs can be used for burrows in orchards, fields, and backyards, they should not be used inside buildings because sparks may be thrown, creating a fire hazard. Groundhogs in buildings or outbuildings should be trapped with live traps baited with apples or other fruits. Then fill in the burrow with rocks to discourage new "squatters."

6

Other Rodent Pests

I n addition to the squirrel family, a number of other rodent pests including mice, rats, voles, gophers, and moles can be real nuisances as well as dangerous. When these critters chew through electrical wires they can cause hazardous shorts. The habits of these rodents are nasty, and they can also carry transmittable diseases. In some situations, rats have become brave enough to bite humans.

Mice and Rats

The house mouse (*Mus musculus*) was brought over from the Old World by the early settlers. Mice have poor vision, but a well-developed sense of smell, taste, and hearing. A female will produce five to eight litters, with each litter averaging five young, in a year. Gestation is only twenty-one days. The young depend on the mother for about three weeks and reach maturity in two to three months. House mice are primarily seed eaters, but they like other foods, particularly sweets. They can live for months on the normal moisture content of seeds and many other foods, but they will readily take water if available. Mice can squeeze

Other common rodent pests include house mice. Mice can squeeze through a hole as small as one-quarter inch.

through holes just a little over a quarter inch in diameter, so it is important that foundations, doors, and windows be frequently inspected and any small openings closed.

The Norway rat (*Rattus norvegius*) weighs about a pound when an adult. The Norway rat is also an Old World rodent and disdainfully called a number of other names, including wharf rat, house rat, barn rat, sewer rat, and black rat. They are about seven to ten inches long with naked scaly tails about another seven to eight inches long. Their ears are fairly short and their fur is a coarse brown with a dirty gray on the underside. They prefer living in close proximity to humans, living in their homes and other buildings and stealing their food. Rats nest in anything from garbage dumps to building foundations—any place they can find a hole. Farmers continually fight rats in their

The Norway rat, another rodent, is extremely comfortable living with humans and can cause extensive damage, as well as present serious health problems.

barns, granaries, silos, and other buildings, but rats are just as comfortable in the city, living in sewers, around wharfs and docks, around slaughterhouses, in warehouses and stores, as well as in the cellars and basements of homes. They're not just nuisances, though. Rats cause millions of dollars of damage each year in food losses alone. They're also carriers of such dread diseases as bubonic plague and typhus, which have caused the deaths of thousands of people.

Rats are primarily nocturnal, except where their populations become extremely high. Rats, like mice, have rather poor eyesight, but more than make up for it with their other senses. They will eat almost anything available and can climb and swim, as well as easily gnaw through many materials. In old houses their nightly gnawing can be a noisy "nightmare." Sign of rats include their droppings as well as gnawed holes in walls and cabinets, door corners, and feed sacks.

Rodent Proofing

The first step in controlling rodents is rodent proofing your home and outbuildings. Rodent proofing involves the use of various construction materials to prevent the movement of rats or mice into or out of a building, room, or given space. The materials used must, in some locations, be impervious to gnawing. In other areas the materials must prevent climbing as a means of entrance.

The upper teeth of rats and mice curve inward, making it difficult, if not impossible, for them to gnaw into a flat, hard surface. For this reason, both critters tend to seek a gnawing edge as a starting point. Edges formed by chipped and indented places or slightly open joints provide a starting point for gnawing. Each small bite of the rodent creates a new edge, and by twisting and turning its head, it forms new holes.

Entry by rats, and to some extent mice, may also be the result of burrowing in the ground beneath foundations and floors. Rats and mice can also climb and enter the upper reaches of structures, or they may go through doors, windows, and other openings. Rodent proofing, to be effective, must take into consideration not only the habits of rats and mice, but human error as well. Mechanical devices to automatically close doors, coupled with other aids that correct human indifference or negligence, must also be used in connection with rodent-proof construction.

Fundamentals of Rodent Proofing

1. Close off all openings more than one-half inch in diameter to prevent access by rats and one-quarter inch in diameter to keep out mice.

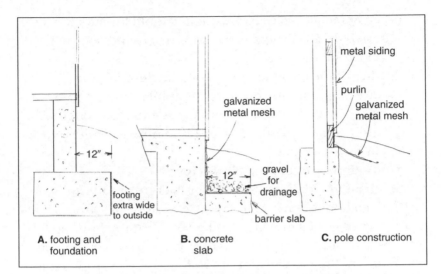

The first step is to rodent proof your house and any outbuildings.

2. Cover all edges that may be subject to gnawing with sheet metal or hardware cloth.

3. Concrete floors and shallow foundations should be constructed with a curtain wall around the outer edge, extending thirty-six inches into the ground, or in an L shape twenty-four inches in the ground with a twelve-inch lip extending outward.

4. Extend rodent proofing to a height of thirty-six inches above the highest probable level of stored or piled materials.

5. Concrete foundations should be at least twelve inches above the ground level to discourage and prevent the gnawing of holes.

6. Sheet metal, twelve inches high, should be smoothly inserted on all corners above floor or ground level to prevent climbing.
7. Check holes around pipes. Force a piece of heavy hardware cloth into the opening, then fill around it with concrete, or use STUF-FIT. Where pipes enter a wooden wall, fit sheet metal flashing around the pipe and anchor it securely to the wall.
8. Install devices to keep doors closed.
9. Fill all foundation cracks with concrete or mortar.
10. Keep floor drains tightly fastened to stop entry from sewers.
11. To rat proof a granary or other outbuilding housing feed that is not built of metal siding, use a skirt of half-inch wire netting to a height of two feet or more from the top of the foundation. Then fasten an eight-inch-wide strip of sheet metal flashing at the top edge of the mesh wire. Use galvanized sheet metal to cover the edges of the door and frame.

Discouraging Rats and Mice

Mice may be brought into the house in sacks of garden produce stored outside, or even stored in the garage and then carried into the house. Mice may also be brought indoors in opened sacks of pet food stored outside. Store any food items, such as pet food or livestock feed, in covered metal or hard plastic containers.

Close all necessary openings, such as windows, doors, and ventilators, with quarter-inch mesh hardware cloth. Keep all doors closed when not in use. Use a good spring or doorkeeper to make sure the door closes and stays closed.

Store materials in basements and cellars on stands at least ten to twelve inches above the floor and on shelves with metal legs. Do not allow litter to accumulate on the floor behind a sink, stove, or cabinet. Set these items flush against the wall, or far enough away so that the space can be easily cleaned.

Do not pile wood near or against building walls. Do not allow weeds and brush to grow against walls. Steps leading into the house should be made of concrete or masonry. If steps are made of wood, the space beneath the steps should be kept open and clean. Keep stored materials such as lumber, pipe, and so forth up off the ground, leaving a space of twelve to eighteen inches. Incidentally, this will also provide fewer living quarters for other critters such as snakes and spiders.

Ultrasonic Devices

The same ultrasonic devices used to deter squirrels and other creatures can also be used to deter mice and rats. Make sure you purchase units that are designed for and have a frequency for these species.

Getting Rid of Rats and Mice

Regardless of your rodent-proofing tactics, you may still end up with mice and rats. The only solution then is to eliminate the pest. Many a youngster in the past has honed his shooting skills with a .22, picking off rats in the light of a flashlight at night at the local garbage dump. In rural areas, shooting may still be a legal option. Unfortunately, the nighttime foray of rats makes even this not an easy chore.

Trapping is a very practical way to remove rats and mice. Trapping is a particularly useful method where the exposure of poisons might be hazardous or where odors from dead rodents may result. A number of different types of manufactured

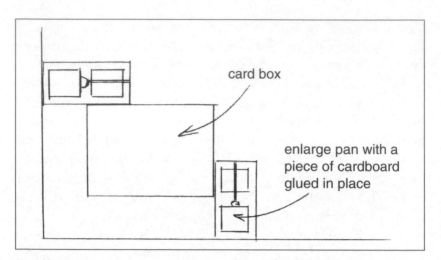

card box

enlarge pan with a
piece of cardboard
glued in place

Trapping with snap or live traps is a very common method of removing mice and rats from premises. Place traps in areas mice inhabit. Determine this by sprinkling suspect areas with flour and looking for tracks. Using obstacles to force mice and rats to use runways with traps and placing boxes over the traps can increase success.

rattraps and mousetraps are readily available. One of the most effective and versatile is the snap trap, which catches the rodent by the neck and kills it when the trap snaps shut. These are available in sizes for both mice and rats. The trap is usually baited, and a wide variety of foods make tempting lures. Peanut butter, nutmeats, doughnuts, cake, fresh fried bacon, cheese, raisins, strawberry jam, and soft candies, particularly milk chocolate and gumdrops, are all good choices. Traps may also be baited by sprinkling rolled oats over and around the bait trigger. If possible, baits should be fastened to the trap by winding a short piece of thread or string around the bait and trigger. Where food is plentiful and nesting material is scarce, good results can sometimes be obtained with cotton tied to the trigger. Hiding the entire trap under a layer of flour, dirt, sawdust, fine shavings, or similar materials may catch even the most trap-shy rodent.

The common wooden-based snap trap can be made more effective by enlarging the bait pan with a piece of heavy cardboard. Cut the cardboard into a square smaller than the guillotine wire and glue it to the existing bait pan with epoxy. To bait the trap, smear a small dab of peanut butter in the center of the enlarged trigger or sprinkle rolled oats over the entire surface. This works well on both rattraps and mousetraps placed where the animals commonly run.

It is extremely important to position traps across the paths that are normally used by mice and rats. If their runways cannot be readily determined, sprinkle a light layer of talcum powder, flour, or similar material in foot-square patches in likely sites. Place traps in the areas where tracks appear. Since rats and mice like to run close to walls, these spots should be checked first and traps set against walls at a 90-degree angle with the pan close to the wall.

You can also use boxes or other obstacles to force the rodent to pass over the trigger. Two or more traps set close together produce better results where many mice or rats are present or where trap-shy critters are a problem. Use plenty of traps rather than rely on one or two to do the job. Due to the short distances normally traveled by mice, place traps within a space of ten feet.

To protect other animals and small children, a trap box can be built to cover the trap. Where the animals travel on rafters or pipes, nail the traps in place or fasten them to small platforms clamped to the pipes. Leave traps in position a few days before moving them to other locations if no critters are caught.

Rats and mice are accustomed to human odors. It is not necessary to boil traps or handle them with gloves. Due to the possibility of disease, however, dead animals, especially rats, and the traps used to catch them should be handled with latex gloves

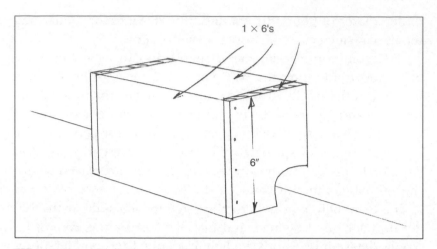

1 × 6's

6"

When using rodenticides, place them under or in bait stations to reduce their hazards and cause mice and rats to use them more readily.

and the gloves properly disposed of. The scent of dead individuals does not deter other rodents. The traps should be checked regularly and kept adjusted to a fine setting.

An alternative method of trapping involves a sticky substance similar to fly paper. This is an effective supplementary method to snap traps, but dust and debris will clog the paper and the tackiness may disappear in a week or less in cold weather. This material is spread on a square of tar paper or heavy cardboard. Usually, bait is placed in the center and the squares are laid in the active runways. As rats and mice become entangled, they can be killed, rolled up in the paper, and disposed of.

Poisons

Poisons have traditionally been used to kill mice and rats. Poisons may be purchased in bulk and mixed in with food as bait, or purchased as ready-made bait stations. The latter are useful for minor infestations. In the past anticoagulant poisons such as Warfarin, Pival, Fumarin, Diphacinone, and PMP have been quite common. These poisons prevent the normal clotting of blood and cause rats and mice to die by internal bleeding.

All of these poisons are available in the form of ready-made baits. Some may also be purchased as concentrates for home-made mixtures. A number of more effective products that also kill by anticoagulant action have been developed. Anticoagulant poisons are capable of killing cats, dogs, and other warm-blooded animals and may be harmful or fatal if swallowed by humans. It is extremely important to follow manufacturers' instructions on their use as well as their hazards.

Regardless, no known rodenticide is completely safe to use. Even those rodenticides considered less hazardous to humans and domestic animals may, under certain conditions, cause death. Although today many poisons come in pellet form in tear-open bait stations, placement of all poisons under a protective cover can reduce their hazards and will also provide the cover preferred by rats and mice when feeding. In addition, bait stations protect the bait from adverse weather and simplify the job of placing baits. Bait stations are particularly useful in exposing anticoagulant baits that must be made continuously available to rats and mice for extended periods.

Bait stations must be sturdily made of solid material in order to avoid being knocked about or crushed by heavy objects being dropped or placed on them. Open bottoms are preferred because rats are more willing to enter boxes that are set on the surfaces they are accustomed to walking on.

A bait station can easily be made from a one-by-twelve-inch board, with openings no larger than three inches in diameter and circular in shape cut in each end. They are easily cut with a saber or band saw.

Rats are always on the alert to their enemies, whether they be predatory birds, dogs, cats, or humans. They prefer an environment that provides convenient cover to which they can scurry when danger threatens. When necessary, rats will travel considerable distances to obtain food, but they prefer to dig burrows and otherwise establish themselves near their food sources. If rats are feeding some distance from their harbors, bait stations should be located along their routes of travel to provide convenient stopovers for protective cover and feeding.

House mice normally maintain their colonies near a food source and seldom range more than a few feet from their living quarters. Bait stations for house mice should be placed in close proximity to their colonies with no more than ten to fifteen feet between them. Where only mice are involved, a suitable bait station can be made by cutting small openings in the side of a small cardboard box such as a shoebox.

Outside Rodents

Occasionally deer mice and other "outside" mice and rats can also become a problem, especially in outbuildings. Deer mice took over our greenhouse several years ago. We thought the greenhouse was totally varmint proof, but one morning I discovered a full flat of petunias nibbled down to the soil. The next morning another flat was gone. Out came the rattraps and poison. Seven dead deer mice later and our greenhouse was safe. We still don't know how they got in.

Meadow mice, also called meadow voles, are small, short, and chunky animals of about seven inches, with a tail less than two inches in length. Voles are ground-dwelling rodents that prefer

Deer mice and other "outdoor" rodents can cause extensive damage. They also tunnel deep underground to eat the tree roots in your orchards. Evidence is often tunnels under the snow.

grassy and weedy areas with lots of rank growth of succulent plant materials. Orchards, hay fields, and weedy fencerows are favored spots. These mice will, however, readily invade lawns, gardens, and nurseries, where they can become serious nuisances. Evidence of meadow mice includes surface runways with overhanging vegetation. These travel lanes will be about one and a half inches wide. Mouse droppings and freshly cut vegetation are also signs. Meadow mice also frequently travel in tunnels beneath the snow. Herbaceous weeds, native grasses, and legumes make up their regular diet, but they will often eat ornamental shrubbery, vegetables, flowers, and bulbs when normal vegetation is scarce. Meadow mice particularly like to chew on the bark of fruit trees, especially apple, and they will often completely girdle a tree, killing it, or in the case of tree seedlings, may eat the tree off completely. Meadow mice also live in deep underground tunnels and can damage orchards by eating the tree roots.

Barriers

The first step in preventing meadow mouse problems in orchards, trees, and ornamentals is to keep high vegetation at least two feet away. This can be done by mowing, herbicide applications, cultivation, or the use of a layer of crushed stone or gravel up to three inches deep. Keep the grass mowed fairly short. Scrape all dead vegetation away from the trees since this provides cover and nesting materials.

Wire guards constructed of three-eighths-inch wire formed into cylinders around trees can help prevent damage from field mice as well as from rabbits and squirrels. The cylinders should be eighteen to twenty-four inches high and about six inches in diameter, or at least three inches larger overall than the diameter of the tree stem.

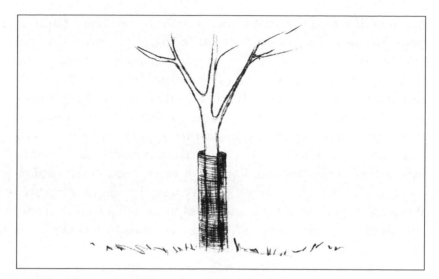

Tree guards or wire cylinders around trees can help prevent field mice and cotton rats from chewing on the bark of young trees.

Trapping

Mouse snap traps can also be used to trap meadow mice. Place the traps at burrow openings, in or near runways, near ornamental shrubbery, flowerbeds, gardens, or rock walls. Bait the traps with rolled oats or a piece of fresh apple. Place the traps so that the trigger pan lays across the runway and then cover the trap with leaves or grass. A small cardboard box with holes in the sides can also be used to cover the trap. Check each morning and evening and re-bait and reset the trap until you do not catch any more mice.

Rodenticides

For larger scale operations, such as orchards and nurseries, a rodenticide may be needed. The most effective method is hand-baiting mouse runs and holes with treated baits. Bait stations can also be made from discarded beverage cans. Cut the end out of a can to about one and a half inches in diameter. Dent or flatten one side of it and place the bait inside. Place the can in a mouse run or hole, flattened side down, and cover with grasses or leaves. Mark the locations of the can with a flag or stake. This method protects the bait from the weather as well as from desirable wildlife. Place one container for each eighty square feet of nursery bed. For larger operations, broadcasting baits selectively into mouse cover may be more effective. Whichever method you choose, apply rodenticides only when several days of fair weather are predicted. Rain and snow cause the baits to lose their effectiveness.

Yard Sharks

Moles and shrews can also do a great deal of damage to lawns as well as gardens. Small animals that spend their lives in underground burrows, moles feed on insects, snails, spiders, small vertebrates, earthworms, and their favorites, white grubs. Shrews are also insectivorous and eat little vegetation. Although moles don't eat much vegetation, their tunneling can be quite vexing. The upturned soil ridges make it hard to mow lawns, and the subterranean bulldozers kill the grass in the disturbed areas. Shrews and meadow mice both use these convenient underground tunnels. Unless moles become a serious hazard, consider their feeding on insects and other soil organisms as beneficial. Before eradicating them, bear in mind that you may create an even more troublesome insect problem in the long run.

If you're really serious about stopping mole problems, you can eliminate their food source with insecticides. This will take some time and will likely kill earthworms and discourage birds from visiting your backyard as well. Many chemical soil treatments are available to kill grubs and other soil organisms. Check with local garden supply stores in your area.

Barriers

Small areas such as flowerbeds can be protected with sheet metal barriers buried in the ground to at least twelve inches to prevent moles and other critters from burrowing. Sonic wave repellers, driven by batteries, are also available for driving away moles and other ground-burrowing critters. One of the better models, although a bit more costly, is solar powered. The easiest and most humane ways of ridding your yard of moles, however, is with a wind-driven lawn fan that creates a constant vibration in the ground. Mole and gopher repellents containing castor oil, a substance moles can't stand, are also available for driving out moles.

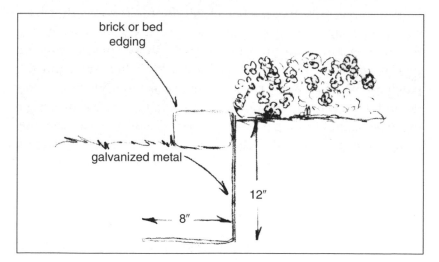

Sheet metal barriers buried at least twelve inches underground can protect small flowerbeds from field mice and moles.

Trapping

Moles are quite often trapped using specially designed traps, including choker and harpoon types. Both types of traps are available through garden centers and farm supply stores. Follow the manufacturer's directions for their specific use. Moles use runways continually, so it's important to determine the active ones. Stomp down on the runways at short intervals. Moles will repair the ones they are using. The abandoned runways will not be repaired.

Once you locate a runway that has been repaired, again stomp down with your heel on a fairly straight section of the runway. This will create an obstruction or cave-in of the runway. Set the trap according to the manufacturer's instructions. Test it a time or two to make sure it is working properly. Then place it down over the caved-in location. When the mole comes to repair the obstruction, the trap will spring.

If the trap does not catch a mole, the mole may either have abandoned the runway or be bypassing the trap. To determine if the mole is still using the runway, use a sharp stick to punch a hole on either side of the trap. Moles don't like light and will patch up the holes in any runway they are using. If the mole plugs the holes but the trap has not been sprung, the mole is simply going around the trap. Again, break down the tunnel with the heel of your foot and reset the trap. If the holes are not plugged and the trap is still not sprung, the trap needs to be relocated.

Poisons

Several poisons are on the market for moles as well. These toxic baits are commonly made in the form of pellets and are placed in the runways according to the manufacturer's directions. You can also place some of them around the edges and throughout a freshly dug flowerbed to prevent loss of bulbs and plants.

Gophers

Pocket gophers (family Geomyidae) are chunky burrowers that are close in size to rats. They have under-slung jaws and external fur-lined cheek pouches in which they carry food. Their curved upper incisors are outside when the mouth is closed, and these, along with their clawed forefeet, are perfectly adapted for digging—and digging is what they do best. Their head is fairly large, but with small ears and eyes. The majority of their lives are spent underground in their burrows. Gophers create a fan-shaped mound, while a mole creates a rounder mound. The tunnel beneath a mole mound extends straight down while that of the gopher leads down at an angle. For the most part, gophers are quite beneficial. Their digging keeps the soil fertile and porous. They do, however, eat bulbs, roots, and other vegetation and their tunneling can also create problems in lawns and other areas. The pocket gophers include the yellow-faced pocket gopher, Plains pocket gopher, northern pocket gopher, and Botta's pocket gopher.

A wide range of products are available for controlling gophers, including Gopher Purge Repellent, Mole-Gopher Repellent, the Black Hole Gopher Trap, and Gopher Gasser. The latter consists of smoke or gas bombs that are lighted and dropped into the gopher's tunnel. Smoke 'Em Bombs are registered by the USDA for control of pocket gophers, ground wasps, moles, woodchucks, and other tunneling garden and lawn pests. The bombs are dropped into the tunnels, where they generate sulfur smoke.

Small Mammals

A number of small mammals can also become nuisances in gardens, outbuildings, and crawl spaces of some homes. Some can also create serious health hazards as well.

Rabbits

Cottontail rabbits love carrots and peas as much as we do. They also love many other garden, flower, lawn, and orchard plants. Rabbits can seriously damage fruit trees and the young saplings of other trees by chewing the bark off the trunks in the winter. Tree trunk guards of one-quarter-inch mesh hardware cloth about eighteen to twenty-four inches high and set into the ground surrounding the trunk can be used to protect trees. Multi-stemmed shrubs can be encircled with hardware cloth for protection. Commercial tree wraps and plastic guards, available from garden centers and horticultural supply houses, can be used. Keep in mind that any tree or shrub guard should be higher than the average snowfall since these small animals can eat from the top of crusted snow. Sonic and chemical repellents are also effective on rabbits, as are low electric fences. Rabbits can also be shot where local laws permit, and according to state game and fish laws. Live trapping is an alternative as well; however, it does little good to live-trap in the summer months when the animals are producing litters of young and plenty of food is available.

Skunks

Skunks are for the most part nocturnal. They are quite secretive and rarely a problem. Skunks feed on fruits, berries, bulbs, and insects, including grubs. They often dig cone-shaped holes in lawns and pastures to get at the grubs. Skunks can, however, become pesky nuisances if they invade homes or outbuildings. In addition to their not-so-nice odor, skunks also can carry rabies. To keep them out, create barriers against entrance into homes and outbuildings. All ground-level openings in building foundations and openings beneath crawl spaces should be sealed with concrete, sheet metal, or heavy wire. If skunks are already occupying a building, close off all openings except one, then check the remaining opening after dark. Use an artificial tracking aid such as lime, flour, or talcum powder at the opening to determine if the animal is inside or has exited the building. If the animal leaves tracks showing it has left the building, you can seal off the opening. Do not seal off openings in May or June, even if you do see tracks exiting the building. The skunks may have young left in the building and they can starve and die.

If a skunk wanders into your garage, workshop, or other outbuilding, don't attempt to chase it out. Instead, leave the door open, and chances are it will wander back out on its own after dark. Sometimes skunks fall into basement or crawl space window wells and can't get out. Place a walkway down into the window well for the skunk to exit. Make the walkway of a rough-sawn board with cleats tacked on the top edge.

To prevent skunks from bothering beehives, place the hives on stands several feet off the ground with sheet metal barriers around the legs of the stand.

Skunks can be live-trapped, but enclosed traps should be used to discourage the animal from releasing its scent. Specially designed, all-metal traps are available commercially for skunks. If using a wire trap, cover it with an old rug or blanket and handle it gently during transport to a release site. Skunks are considered furbearers by most fish and game departments. Before trapping or killing, contact your local fish and game department for rules and regulations. Because of the danger of rabies and the consequences of getting sprayed by Mr. Skunk, you may be better off calling a local health department or nuisance-animal control office for help with pesky skunks.

The odor from a skunk is extremely strong and long lasting, and it's also extremely difficult to neutralize. Ammonia, bleach, vinegar, and canned tomatoes or tomato juice all work to some degree. Commercial deodorants are also available from pest-control operators.

Raccoons and Possums

With a penchant for everything from ripening sweet corn to fruits and pet food, both of these small mammals can become real nuisances. More than one pet owner has found a possum sleeping in their pet food sack or barrel. The first step is to keep pet food in covered metal or hard plastic containers. Keep garbage in covered containers as well. The same basic steps of garden and orchard prevention can be used with these animals as well. We regularly use a low-voltage hot wire to protect our garden.

Live trapping is a good method of controlling these pests. Bait the trap with canned fish (any kind that is packed in oil). A fish-based cat food is also effective. If cats are a problem, use peanut butter and honey or molasses mixed half and half for the trapping bait.

7

Lethal Versus Non-lethal

The most effective means of controlling nuisance squirrels is to shoot the offending animals, providing this is in accordance with local ordinances and state game laws. One of the most effective guns for squirrel eradication is the .22 rimfire rifle. Loaded with shorts, the .22 has taken millions of squirrels. Hollow-point shells are even more effective than solids. Remember, however, even relatively low-powered guns such as .22s have long ranges of more than a mile and can be dangerous in populated areas. Extremely low-velocity rimfire cartridges are also available specifically for pest control. These shells have relatively short ranges and are also fairly quiet, creating less of a disturbance in suburban areas. Keep in mind that even these low-velocity cartridges may not be legal in some areas. Another alternative is to use .22 rimfire shotshells, which have a very limited range. They can, however, be effective on small animals such as ground squirrels at close ranges, but may simply wound larger animals. These shotshells can be a last-minute resort for exterminating animals inside buildings, but will still do some damage. It's also important to wear safety glasses when using these shells in enclosed areas.

Where and when it is legal, one of the most effective means of controlling nuisance squirrels and other pests is shooting them.

Growing up as a farm kid, pest control was a favorite pastime. Many a winter night was spent stalking English sparrows in my granddad's chicken house or in the thick cedar trees of my dad's homestead. You had to be quiet in the chicken house or the chickens would become alarmed, and nothing is more raucous than a houseful of excited chickens squawking, wings flapping, with dust and droppings flying everywhere. And, Granddad didn't want his chickens disturbed; he just wanted the sparrows eliminated.

The preferred method was simple: a flashlight and a BB gun. My first BB gun was a Daisy Red Ryder model. This nighttime hunting was also a lot more fun with two people—one to hold the flashlight and one to do the shooting. Of course, we traded off with success. My dad also taught my brother the skills early on, and then it was just my brother and me.

Pellet and BB Guns

House sparrows can be real nuisances on farms and in hunting camps. They don't migrate, and on cold winter nights they like to tuck in under the eaves of farm and rural outbuildings. Although the pests hate to leave the comfort of their roosts, and often sit tight in the light, they can be jittery, especially after a few nights of being hassled. Quiet, slow stalking of known roost areas presents the best opportunities. Shooting distance is usually five to fifteen feet, just right for a BB gun—and BBs don't damage wooden structures. Air guns are available in a wide range of prices and styles from semi-automatic CO_2-powered models and quite expensive tournament-style target guns to very economical single-shot models. For economical pest control the Crosman 1760 CO_2 single shot, bolt-action rifle is a good choice. It utilizes .177 pellets, creating a velocity of 700 fps.

That's more than enough to take down sparrows, starlings, and other barn and outbuilding pests, including rats, mice, and even gophers. Pump-action air rifles allow you to control the fps to some degree, with more velocity with more pumps. The Benjamin & Sheridan .177 pellet bolt-action pump air rifle can produce up to 800 fps. If you like handgunning, you may wish to consider any one of the Crosman or Benjamin & Sheridan air pistols not only for safe pest control, but also for great plinking fun as well. Always wear shooting safety glasses.

Rimfire and Centerfire Shotshells

Another excellent choice for short-range pest control is rimfire shotshells. They're available from Winchester, Remington, and Federal as well as CCI. The CCI pellets are contained in plastic capsules for better patterns and cleaner barrels. CCI also manufactures a shotshell for the popular .22 magnum. If you want to use your favorite handgun for short-range pest control, CCI Blazer ammunition is available in a wide range of calibers, including a .45 Colt load. The Blazer .45 Colt shotshells contain No. 9 shot, the optimum size for good pellet energy without sacrificing pattern integrity, with a polyethylene over-powder cup wad that provides a tight gas seal and clean performance. It is loaded in the brand's exclusive, strong aluminum cases designed for both economy and smooth feeding in semi-autos. The shotshell fits standard .45 Colt revolver chambers for reliable function and easy extraction. The case conforms to the dimensions of conventional .45 Colt ammunition.

For larger pests, but still relatively short range, one gun/ammunition combo that's hard to beat is the Thompson/Center Encore .410 pistol. I've used it to dispatch groundhogs, skunks, and possums around my farm. It's a single-shot, break-open de-

A wide variety of guns and ammunition, including rimfire and centerfire, as well as pellet guns can be used.

sign that's quick and easy to load and packs the punch of a regular .410 load.

Safety

Pellets can dent and sometimes go right through a metal-sided or metal-roofed building, especially if the more powerful air guns are used. The larger caliber centerfire shotshell hand-gun loads can also damage these buildings, especially at short ranges. It's a good idea to make a test shot in an area where damage won't be noticed. Outside of buildings, however, any of these offer excellent pest control that, due to their short range, is safe in fairly populated areas. You must, however, use all safety precautions and make sure of what's behind your target.

If shooting in buildings, make sure you wear shooting safety glasses to protect your eyes from possible ricochets. When firing the larger caliber handguns, always wear ear protection as well. Remington M-31 earmuffs have a noise rating of 31, the highest rated hearing protection in the world, yet weigh only ten ounces and are extremely comfortable.

Regardless of your pest problems, there's a safe method of controlling them with today's guns and specialty ammunition. And, you may discover or rediscover a time-honored tradition many a farm youngster cherishes.

Steel Traps

Kill trapping, or trapping with traps designed to kill the animal caught, is also very effective pest control. This, however, can be dangerous to other species, including pets. Kill trapping should be used only as a last resort, and only in places where pets don't have access to the traps. Live trapping may be the best choice.

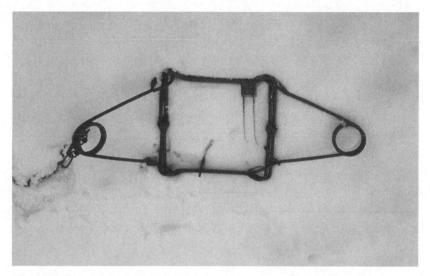

In cases where live trapping and relocation are not allowed, kill trapping may be required. This must, however, be done in places where children and pets do not have access to the traps. Shown is a Conibear trap.

Some counties and cities, however, do not allow live trapping and relocation. Any animal caught must then be destroyed on location or taken to local animal control offices to be destroyed. Make sure you follow local ordinances and state game trapping laws.

The most commonly used killer traps are the Conibear 110 and Conibear 55 bodygripper traps. These traps kill the animal instantly by crushing either its body or head. Conibear traps are commonly used by wildlife control officers, as well as fur trappers trapping mink, beaver, or muskrats. These traps should be positioned on rooftops or near openings, in runways in attics, and other places squirrels inhabit but where pets and children can't get to. These types of traps are commonly not baited, but placed directly in the runway. When the animal goes through them, the trap is sprung. A little bait, such as Pecan Paste, from U-Spray, Inc., along with a handful of peanuts or sunflower seeds placed in the runway, however, can be an added entice-ment. Regardless of where located, these traps must be solidly anchored in place. They come with a chain and ring that can be fastened with a large screw to any wood surface. Care must be used in setting the traps. They slam shut with a great deal of force and can injure your hand if caught. Again, these types of traps should not be used in any location where children can get at them.

Chipmunks can be caught in snap-type rattraps. Place these in runs the little critters use. Place a pair of traps at 90 degrees, facing in toward the path used.

Electrocution Traps

Electrocution devices designed to kill rodents can also be used to kill ground squirrels and flying squirrels. Powered by batteries, these devices will kill any small rodent that enters and grounds itself out. U-Spray, Inc. suggests using their Pecan Paste along with a few sunflower seeds placed in the back of the trap to lure the rodent inside. Once the animal enters and contacts two metal plates, an electric current is generated for thirty to sixty seconds, long enough to hu-manely kill the critter. The dead squirrel is easily removed, and a switch is flicked to reset the trap. These are also excel-lent devices for use in attics and other interior spots. They can be used outside, but must be protected from the weather. Although the shock from the device is not lethal to children and large pets, it can hurt and should not be used in any loca-tion pets or children have access to.

Poisons

Rat poisons can also be used on the smaller members of the squirrel family, but like steel traps, they are non-selective. There is a very distinct possibility of killing your or your neighbor's favorite pet. Poisons of any type should not be used in any area where children have access.

Live Trapping

Live trapping is a very effective way of removing a few nuisance animals without destroying them, and may be the only method recommended for areas where shooting is prohibited. Live trapping, however, is quite controversial, and has its positive and negative aspects.

Live trapping is considered trapping, just as using leg-hold or killer steel traps, and all local ordinances and state game and fish regulations must be followed.

Types of Live Traps

Live traps are commonly wire cages that allow the animal to see through them. A wide variety of sizes are available commercially. An 18-x-6-x-6-inch size is appropriate for small squirrels such as chipmunks and ground squirrels. Tree squirrels, rabbits, and muskrats will require a larger, 24-x-8-x-8-inch size. For raccoons and skunks you'll need an even larger 36-x-12-x-12-inch-size trap. For beaver and woodchucks a 48-x-16-x-16-inch trap is best. The larger traps can also be used for the smaller animals to some extent. The trip pan tension on the larger traps, however, must be adjusted for the lighter weight of the smaller animal.

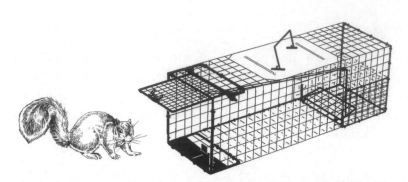

Live trapping and relocation may be the best choice in some situations and areas. The most common manufactured traps are wire cages. (Drawing courtesy Kness Traps)

It's a good idea to purchase a trap that will catch the largest animal you intend to trap. Cage traps are available at many local hardware, farm supply, and sporting goods stores. These traps are also available through mail order from several companies listed in the sources at the back of the book. Some city animal control agencies may also have cage traps for rent or loan, and they're also available from some local rental companies.

Cage traps are available in two types: single entrance and dual entrance. A single-entrance trap has only one opening to allow the animal to enter the trap. In most instances, a door closes behind the animal once it enters the trap. In some instances, the trap is designed to prevent the animal from exiting back through the open door. A double-entrance trap has both a front and a rear door. The trip pan design also differs between the two types of traps. On single-entrance traps, the trip pan is located at the rear of the trap. On double-door traps, the trip pan is located in the center. Double-door traps are also longer than single-door traps to allow for the trip pan location. Double-entrance traps are not commonly multiple-catch traps, enabling you to catch a continuing number of critters. The advantage they offer is being able to position the trap with both doors open on a trail in order to catch the animal whether coming or going. Double-entrance traps, naturally, are more expensive.

In addition to the standard cage traps, several specialty traps are available for catching skunks, snakes, and birds. The latter two are commonly repeat-catch traps, allowing you to make multiple catches. Special "clam shell"-type live traps are also available for beaver as well.

Using Cage Traps

In most instances, the traps will come from the manufacturer adjusted to suit the animal it was designed to catch. Manufacturers usually include a user's guide as well for adjusting the trap for other animals or to readjust after extended use. Trip-pan adjustment is extremely important. The adjustment should not be so light it trips at the least movement of the trap or even the wind. On the other hand, the trip-pan adjustment should not be so heavy the animal can't trip it when the trip pan is touched. Animals learn very quickly. It's best to catch the nuisance animal on the first try and not "educate" the critter with a miss. In most instances, the trip pan should be set for one-quarter-pound pressure for squirrels. The same pressure will also catch rabbits. For larger critters such as raccoons and woodchucks, the pressure should be between one-half and one pound. For even larger animals such as coyotes, the pressure will range up to three pounds. Locate an object of the required weight to help in adjusting the trip-pan tension, or follow the manufacturer's directions. The main factor is to make sure the trip pan and door are free to move and are not binding in any manner.

Although some general rules must be followed, specific tactics are used for trapping the various nuisance animals, including squirrels. The most important factor in success with live trapping is a thorough knowledge of the critter's habits. Being able to read sign, or the evidence left by the critter, will tell you what the animal is and where and how to set the trap. Learn to identify the tracks, droppings, and evidence of gnawing, feeding, and other habits. The single key to any trapping success is to place the trap where animals want to be for some reason or other, whether a travel lane, feed source, or denning area. Traps set in travel lanes or trails used by animals are the most successful. Double-entrance traps can be set directly in the trail. Single-entrance traps must be set off to the side, but right next to the trail. If setting live traps near denning or nesting areas, don't set them directly at the opening since this may alarm the animal. Instead, set the trap a slight distance away.

It is extremely important to secure live traps. This not only prevents the animal from rolling the trap over and possibly escaping, but also deters thieves and vandals. Simply wire or chain the trap to a close-by object. If no suitable object is readily available, drive a stake in the ground and fasten the trap to the stake.

Any type of trapping is a game of patience. You may catch the critter on the first try, but in many instances, it may be a week or several days before you're successful. Don't be afraid to move or reset a trap that isn't successful, especially if you see evidence the animal is still using the area.

Bait

In most instances, live traps are baited to attract the animal. Any number of different baits and commercial lures may be used to bait them. The bait used depends on the specific animal. Baits consist of either food bait or a lure. Food baits are simply foods the animals normally eat. Whole corn, sunflower seeds, and peanuts are examples of prime food baits for squirrels. Scent baits or lures are manufactured products that lure the animal to the trap by the scent. A number of these commercially prepared baits are available for different species of animals. With an extremely wary critter, you may need to set more than one live trap, with different baits in each. Don't overdo the lures; it only takes a tiny bit to attract most animals. Food baits are normally placed at the back of the trap or just behind the pan. Don't place the food bait so close to the trap sides or back that you allow the animal to reach in and steal the bait. In some cases you may, however, have to place a bit of food just inside the front door to entice the animal to visit the trap. Placing some bait in this location and some behind the trap is especially effective. For an extremely wary animal, keep the trapdoor closed and place the food just outside. Once the animal becomes accustomed to the free handout, move the bait to inside the trap. Again, you may have to start out with the food just inside the door at first. Fasten the door so that it can't close and gradually move the bait farther to the back of the trap. Once the animal becomes accustomed to entering the trap with no reaction, you can set the trap with the food just behind the pan.

Concealment

Since live traps are not natural to the animal's habitat, they are also often concealed to further dupe the critter. The concealment used should be native to the area. Use grass and weeds in a grassy backyard; in wooded areas use leaves and brush for trap concealment. It's also a good idea to place bits of camouflaging material on the floor of the trap as well, but make sure

Live traps take some "learning" to use. They should be concealed, and quite often bait is used to entice the squirrel or rodent into the trap.

this material doesn't interfere with the trip-pan operation, or the closing of the door. Many animals readily investigate a hole, especially the burrowing animals.

In some instances, such as a rooftop trap set for squirrels, it's usually not possible to conceal the trap. Animals in these types of urban environments, however, are usually not as wary as their wilder cousins.

Checking Traps

Check your trap regularly. The best tactic is to check the trap at least twice a day. Check it first thing each morning, as many animals are primarily nocturnal or diurnal. Then check the trap again in late afternoon, just before the evening hours. Regardless of the time, always check the trap within every twenty-four hours. Leaving an animal in a cage trap is cruel and should be avoided if at all possible. A pair of binoculars can often be used to check the trap from a distance. Check to see if the door is closed. If not, has the bait been removed?

If you see the trapdoor has been sprung, approach the trap slowly. Most animals quickly become alarmed at the scent and sight of an approaching human while contained in a trap. In their fear, they may injure themselves.

Trapping Specific Animals

The previous information covers the generalities of live trapping. Following are more specific details for trapping various nuisance species.

Squirrels

Both tree and ground squirrels are fairly easy to live-trap. Use corn, sunflower seeds, or raw peanuts as bait. Squirrels are quite curious and will often inspect a new item in their territory. Since they live in close proximity to humans, many urban and suburban squirrels are quite unafraid as well. Set traps to take advantage of the nuisance squirrels' habits. For instance, if they're nesting in your attic, set the trap in the attic. Just remember to check the trap frequently. Bait with the foods most common in your area. By the same token, if squirrels are raiding your bird feeder, place bird feed in the trap and set it near or under the feeder. If squirrels are digging up your lawn to bury nuts, bait the trap with nuts or nutmeats and place it near a tree in your yard. Ground squirrels are best trapped near nest sites.

Woodchucks

Since woodchucks use burrows in the ground, simulating a burrow by covering the trap with a tarp can be effective. Bait can be almost any type of fresh vegetable, including lettuce, peas, carrot tops, and even fresh fruit. Woodchucks are harder to trap in the spring and early summer months when food is plentiful.

Muskrats

Traps to catch muskrats should be placed near the water's edge of ponds, lakes, and streams. Make sure the trap is well concealed and bait it with corn or fruit. Adding a muskrat lure can add to its effectiveness.

Armadillos

Armadillos can destroy gardens and flowerbeds with their digging. Place traps alongside garden walls, fences, or pathways to their burrows. Boards can be used to funnel an animal into the trap. In most instances, bait is not used.

Cottontail Rabbits

Cottontail rabbits are the easiest animals to trap. Merely set the traps in places where they're creating a nuisance. The trap doesn't even need to be concealed. In gardens, simply place the trap between the rows and bait with lettuce, carrot trimmings, corn, or fresh peas.

Relocation

Nuisance animals may be live-trapped, then dispatched, but in most instances they are relocated to another area. Relocation, however, raises many thorny issues. Many animals are extremely territorial and won't survive in a new territory. Some animals will also succumb from the stress of trapping, transporting, and relocation. And, some may simply become a nuisance in another area. Unless relocated some distance away, others may also simply come back "home." Finding a suitable relocation area may be your biggest problem. Experts suggest relocating a nuisance animal at least ten miles from where it was caught. In most instances, the release site should also not be heavily populated with people. If you're not sure where to release the animal, or even what to do with the animal, contact your local nuisance-animal agencies for help.

Dangers

Trapped wild animals are dangerous. Even the smallest, seemingly timid creature can become a monster when trapped. They can somehow reach through the wire to bite and scratch and the resulting wounds may become infected. In addition, many animals also carry dangerous diseases, some of which can be transmitted to humans. Always wear heavy leather gloves when handling the trap. Placing a cover over the trap often has a calming effect on the animal. Do not attempt to handle the animal in any way. If you wish to leave the trap in place to catch other critters, transfer cages are also available from some manufacturers.

If animals seemed to be weak, sick, or act strange, do not transport them or attempt to release them into another area.

Call a local game and fish department or the animal nuisance agency or local health department. The animal may have a very serious transmittable disease.

Releasing

Many wild critters come out of the cage fighting. To release a trapped animal, place the cage on the ground. Open the door and quickly step behind the cage and some distance away. Do not stand in front of it. In most instances, the animal will quickly escape from the trap and run away. In some instances, however, it may hesitate. Be patient—it will come out eventually.

Home-Built Traps

You can also build your own live traps, suiting them to the specific animal. For instance, rabbit traps are easy to build and use. As a youngster I trapped rabbits for pocket money, selling the rabbits to the local farm store. The rabbits were trapped in wooden box traps. I had about a dozen traps set out on my relatives' farms and caught lots of rabbits, in addition to lots of possums, the occasional skunk, and the one animal I really dreaded, stray cats. The last were madder than hornets when released from the trap. You could hear them snarling even before you reached the trap.

The box trap is a quite simple affair made of scrap lumber. When the animal enters the trap it runs into a peg set in a hole in the top. The peg is knocked from the hole, allowing a door to drop down. For animals that like to check out tunnels, the back is solid. For those animals that frequent trails, a wire mesh back can be used. The size can be adjusted to fit almost any animal. The size shown will accommodate rabbits or squirrels.

Building a Box Trap

Materials:

A. Sides, ¾" × 9¼" × 24", 2 required.

B. Bottom, ¾" × 9¼" × 24", 1 required.

C. Rear top, ¾" × 9¼" × 21½", 1 required.

D. Front top, ¾" × 1½" × 9¼", 1 required.

E. Front outside strips, ¾" × 1½" 9¼", 2 required.

F. Front inside strips, ¾" × 1½" × 9¼", 2 required.

G. Door, ¾" × 7½" × 12", 1 required.

H. Upper support arm, ¾" × 1½" × 12½", 1 required.

I. Rear support arm, ¾" × 1½" × 3", 1 required.

J. Trip arm, ¾" × ¾" × 21", 1 required.

K. Trip, ¾" × ¾" × 9", 1 required.

L. Back, ½" hardware cloth, 9¼" × 12¼", 1 required.

Fasteners:

Staples, ½", 12 required.

Screws, No. 6 × 1½", self-starting wood screws, 36 required.

Screw eyes, 4 required.

String, 36"

Construction:

Begin construction by cutting the bottom and two sides to the proper length. Cut the inner and outer door support strips to the proper length and width. Mark their locations on the sides and fasten them in place with self-starting wood screws. Fasten the bottom to the two sides with self-starting wood screws.

Cut the rear top piece and fasten in place to the sides with self-starting wood screws. Cut the drop door to width and length. Cut the front top piece to width and length, and fasten it in place down on the sides with self-starting wood screws. Make sure it is spaced far enough from the rear top piece so the drop door will drop down easily. Cut the hardware cloth back to the proper size and fasten to the back of the sides, top, and bottom with ½-inch staples.

Cut the upper support arm to the proper width and length. Cut the notch in the top using a handsaw and a chisel. Cut the rear support arm to proper size and width and fasten the upper arm to it with self-starting wood screws. Fasten the support arm assembly to the top of the box with self-starting wood screws. Cut the trip arm to width and length. Bore a ³⁄₁₆-inch hole in the center of the trip arm. Fasten the trip arm in place on the support arm with a small nail driven through the side of the support arm notch, positioned through the hole in the center of the trip arm and then driven into the opposite side of the support arm notch.

Bore the hole for the trip in the top of the box. Cut the trip to size and then whittle the notch and shaped end. Install a screw eye in each end of the trip arm, the upper end of the trip, and the upper end of the drop door.

Place the drop door in the down position and attach an 18-inch length of string to the door eye and the front eye on the trip arm. Tie an 18-inch piece of string to the back trip arm eye and, holding the trip in position in the hole, pull down on the trip arm string until the door slides up and open. Attach the string to the trip eye at that position. Reach in and push the trip arm toward the back to trip the door and drop it. You will have to adjust the length of the strings to get a good, quick drop of the door.

Position the trap where the animal has to go through it on a trail or runway it frequents. Block off other possible tunnels or

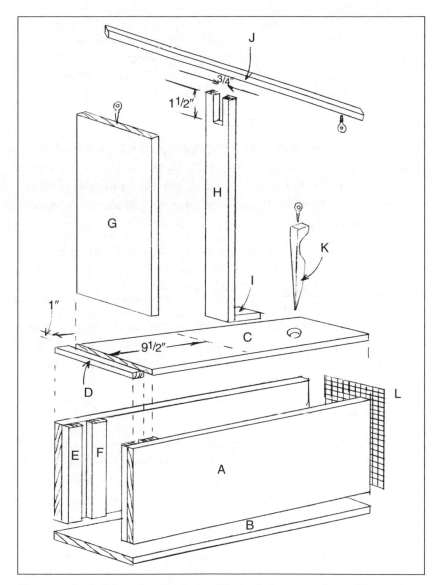

You can also build wooden live traps. The trap shown can be used for squirrels, rabbits, opossums, and even skunks.

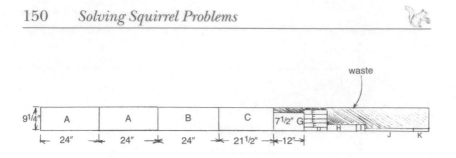

routes. Then place bait in the trap so the animal will have to go past the trip in order to get to the bait. You may have to wait a day or two for the animal to discover the bait and trap. Lettuce or carrots will attract rabbits, corn or nuts will attract squirrels, anything will attract raccoons or possums.

A trap can also be constructed explicitly for squirrels with slightly smaller dimensions and a different type of trip using a pan the animal steps on. The same type of trap can be made larger for other critters as well.

Actually, barrels, buckets, and pipes can also be rigged as live traps. Or you can construct your own cage traps of wood or welded steel; either can be covered with welded wire mesh.

Catchpoles

In some instances, you may simply need to catch a critter and move it outside a building. The Ketch-All Pole from the Ketch-All Company is famous for its versatility. Used by wildlife and humane officers for many years for both domestic and wild animals, the patented Ketch-All Pole affords maximum protection to the handler and humane handling of the animal. It is available in several sizes and can be used successfully on all sizes of animals from squirrels to cougars. Up a tree, under a building, or in a storm drain, the animal can easily and safely be caught

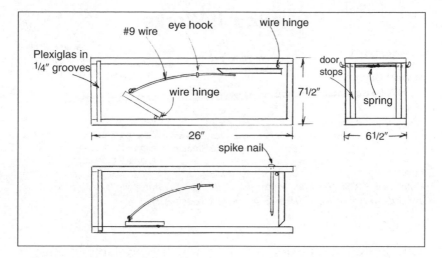

A smaller trap, specifically designed for squirrels and other small rodents, can be used either indoors or outdoors.

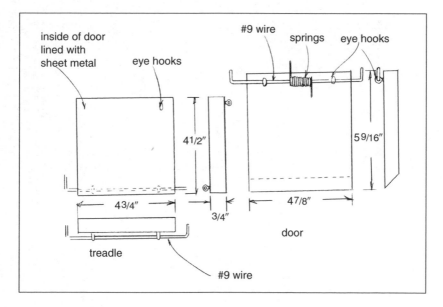

How It Works

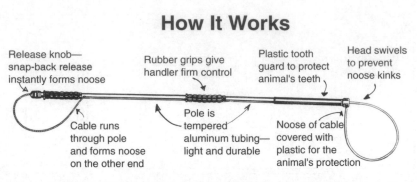

Release knob—
snap-back release
instantly forms noose

Rubber grips give
handler firm control

Plastic tooth
guard to protect
animal's teeth

Head swivels
to prevent
noose kinks

Cable runs
through pole
and forms noose
on the other end

Pole is
tempered
aluminum tubing—
light and durable

Noose of cable
covered with
plastic for the
animal's protection

*Some animals may simply be caught with a special noose such as that used by
animal control officers. (Drawing courtesy Ketch-All)*

with the Ketch-All extension pole, which is available in lengths
up to twelve feet.

Hunting Squirrels

8

I can't help it. When the first hickory leaves begin turning a burnished gold in the fall, I simply have to go squirrel hunting. Two reasons bring me back to a certain grove of hickories each fall: a chance for a pot of squirrel stew and the possibility of hickory nut pie. If I happen to get lucky and get to the woods before the squirrels gather all the nuts, I get the pie, but it seldom happens. Regardless of how closely I watch the little grove, it seems the squirrels swarm in overnight, just as the hickory nuts ripen to prime. All I'm left with are the discards, those with the almost invisible tiny holes in the hulls, indicating a worm-eaten, worthless husk. I've never figured out yet how the little rascals determine the quality of the nutmeats within the shells, but they can sort better than a housewife at a melon stand.

Indeed, one of the best ways of keeping tree squirrels in check is hunting them, where allowed. Make sure you follow local laws regarding hunting as well as state fish and game laws regarding squirrels. Some folks can, however, take this to an extreme, as I discovered in the Ozarks several years ago. I met a fellow, a lone bachelor who lived back in the woods close to one

One of the best ways of keeping squirrels in check, where legal, is hunting them. It's also a tradition with many hunters.

of the Arkansas national forests. He was a bit on the odd side, and I happened to notice that none of the windows on his house had screens. At my comment, he quipped, "Gives me 360-degree coverage of the little varmints." Then I learned he waged an all-out war on the numerous gray squirrels that poured out of the forestland to ravage his garden and orchard. A .22 shot from the windows was his tactic that resulted in a steady diet of fried squirrel.

For most of us, however, squirrel hunting has a different "flavor." Hunting squirrels offers a chance to be in the woods when other hunting seasons are not open. The action is often fast paced, but does require good woodsmanship. Many deer hunters use squirrel hunting before the deer season to brush up on their woodsman and stalking skills, while scouting for deer sign at the same time they hunt squirrels. Squirrel hunting is also a great traditional way of introducing youngsters to the sport of hunting. Once the backbone of early America's hunting culture, squirrel hunting has taken a back seat in recent years to more glamorous game, such as deer and turkey. Yet squirrel hunting still offers plenty of excitement, even to veteran hunters. Best of all, squirrels are abundant over both private and public lands, so there are plenty of opportunities to hunt with very little competition. And, of course, there's the great eating a mess of squirrels can provide. Squirrel season in many parts of the country runs fairly long, from early summer through the early months of winter. Tactics and methods can vary with the seasons.

Summer Squirrels

Clouds of mosquitoes swarm around your face, you imagine armies of ticks and chiggers climbing your legs into your shorts, and a steady stream of sweat runs down your brow and drips from your nose. Having fun yet? You bet! You're enjoying one of the best traditions of many parts of the country—summertime squirrel hunting.

Summertime squirrel hunting is a passion with many for a number of reasons. First is the solitude. You'll most likely be the only person in the woods, as opposed to the fall months when the woods are full of hunters chasing everything from squirrels to turkeys to deer. And, for serious hunters, squirrels are about the only game in town during the summer months.

"Summer squirrel hunting is a great way to keep your deer hunting skills honed during the off season," adds Brad Harris, Public Relations Director for Lohman Mfg Co., renowned deer hunter, and squirrel-hunting "nut."

Summer squirrel hunting is quite a bit different from, the fall months, when the bushytails are concentrated on cutting nuts and all you need to do is find the latest droppings of hickories or acorns. Three popular techniques for hunting summer squirrels include calling, still/stalk hunting, and stump sitting. A hunt I experienced last summer with Brad taught me a whole new summer squirrel-hunting tactic—distress calling. Brad and I slipped into the woods at just about daylight to a spot I thought had only a few squirrels. Brad proceeded to show me that my estimation was wrong—the area was loaded with them. My usual tactic in the past had been the old-time method of slipping in quietly and setting up, then waiting for the squirrels to show. Instead, Brad began to shake a sapling hard enough to whip the limbs to the ground and at the same time squeal and squeak loudly on a wooden call. He just grinned at my frowning gaze, sat quietly for a moment, and then pointed toward a movement as a squirrel scurried from treetop to treetop coming our way—fast. Squirrels then began to come from all directions.

"Back-to-back, and every man for himself," I whispered to Brad with a grin.

Within a half-hour, we had collected half of a limit of squirrels each, and were walking to another spot. "Yeah, it's a heck of a lot of fun," admitted Brad. "The sound produced by the Lohman Mr. B's Distress Squirrel Whistle simulates the distress call of a young squirrel, and shaking the limb makes it sound as if a young squirrel has been knocked off it by an owl or hawk. When other squirrels in the area hear the sound they just go crazy and come right to it. I've had dozens of squirrels come in from all directions."

Brad usually begins his calling routine by shaking the bush vigorously and producing four or five loud whistles. He then pauses, because often squirrels will come in immediately. If not, he'll just barely move the bush or sapling and inhale on the call four or five times to keep them interested. If he doesn't get action within five minutes or so, he's out of there and looking for another spot. According to Brad, the distress call can be used any time of the year, but it's best from spring through late summer when there's good leaf cover. "They really can't see long distances then and you can sneak in on them better," he added.

A more traditional summer squirrel technique is still/stalk hunting. The best time is at daybreak when squirrels come out of their leafy nests to grab breakfast before they head back to sleep away the hot hours of the day. I named this method "stop-and-go" hunting over three decades ago when I sold my first outdoor article. The object is to slip into the woods, hunting into the morning sun and stopping frequently to watch the far horizon treetops for movement. The silhouetted trees make it easy to spot any movement in the uppermost branches, where summer squirrels do most of their foraging. A squirrel or a bird can cause the movement, so a pair of

Still-hunting/stalking is a favored hunting method and a great way to practice woodsmanship.

Another favored tactic is quietly sitting near a favored food source.

lightweight binoculars is handy. Once you've determined it's a squirrel, make a stalk to the tree, keeping other trees between you and the target tree until you can get close enough for a shot. This method of squirrel hunting will surely improve your stalking skills for big game.

The third tactic involves simply plunking your rear down near a tree that you know harbors squirrels and waiting them out. This is a favorite tactic of Jerry Thies, a doctor friend of mine from Osceola, Missouri. Jerry hunts with a .22 rimfire rifle, and it's not unusual for him to take four or five squirrels from the same tree in this fashion. He very carefully makes a shot, marks where the fallen squirrel drops, waits for another to appear, shoots it, and then continues his vigil. "Even after a rifle shot, they'll often reappear within a matter of minutes," Jerry relates. "You just have to have a bit of old-fashioned patience."

The secret to this tactic is to be where the squirrels are, and that means finding the exact tree the squirrels are using. Den trees are favorites and will often produce year after year. This does not mean shooting squirrels out of leaf nests or shooting at nests in hopes of driving the squirrels out. But a big old gnarled oak pockmarked with den holes can hold a good number of squirrels.

Early in the season squirrels feed on the buds and flowers of oaks, maples, elms, and sweet gum trees. In early summer one of the best trees to locate is a mulberry. Find a fruiting mulberry tree, and you're looking at a squirrel version of McDonald's. As the summer progresses squirrels forage on berry crops of bramble fruits, wild cherries, wild plums, and sometimes Osage orange balls.

If you're willing to prepare for the ticks, chiggers, and heat, you'll find summertime squirrel hunting a great sport.

Fall Squirrels

Fall squirrel hunting offers many reasons to be in the woods, as I mentioned at the beginning of this chapter. Squirrels are opportunists, and follow the mast crop beginning with the first ripening nuts throughout the fall until the last nuts drop from the trees. Knowing what is ripening, and where, is the key to a successful fall squirrel hunt. Hickory nuts are not the only preferred nuts. Actually, the first nuts to ripen in many parts of the country are the hazelnuts, those semi-sweet delicious cousins to filberts. But I've only been able to beat the squirrels to my hazelnut patch one season.

This follow-the-mast squirrel tactic makes fall hunting both exceedingly productive and extremely frustrating. If you find the particular nut grove the squirrels are working on at the moment, you can often limit out on bushytails in a hurry. But, finding the right nut patch is the key. Almost all the squirrels in a fairly large area can be concentrated in one small patch, and you can spend a great deal of time searching instead of shooting.

My good friend and hunting buddy Brad explains a good example of the problem and a new tactic to combat it: "Last season I went into an area that always had lots of hickory nuts and held lots of squirrels. But, when I got to my little honey hole, the squirrels had already cut it out. The nuts were all gone and so were the squirrels. I was pretty disappointed, but decided to just start moving through the woods, looking for more nut trees. I also decided I might as well start working a barking squirrel call, kind of like walking and calling for turkeys. So I just began walking and barking on my Lohman Squirrel Call. I would ease through the trees, stop and bark a minute or two, then move on. I finally got some squirrels barking a couple of ridges away,

Calling squirrels is also extremely productive at times.

slipped over, and found them cutting up a storm. The squirrels had simply moved with the availability of the nuts.

"Normally I hunt with a .22 rifle, but that day I was hunting with a shotgun. I got under a tree that had eight or nine squirrels in it, really cutting hard on the scaly bark hickory nuts. I dumped one, another ran and I dumped him, then of course they all shut up. I didn't move and I didn't go after the squirrels I had just shot, but marked where each squirrel had hit the ground.

"Then I brought out my secret weapon, the Lohman Squirrel Cutter Call. I started imitating the sound squirrels make when they are cutting or eating nuts. At that time of the year they're in a feeding frenzy; they just eat, eat, and eat constantly, and then they lay up and eat some more. So when an old squirrel hears that cutting sound, they think another squirrel is cutting nuts. It just drives them crazy, and they move immediately to beat the other squirrel to the food.

"I ended up dumping my limit, six squirrels, out of that one tree. Every time I shot they would stop and lock up on the limbs. They would lie very still and look and look and look, but I didn't move, just kept on cutting. What started out as a bust hunt ended up as one of my most exciting hunts."

If you know the woods, you can locate squirrels simply by following the mast. In my part of the country, the first mast is hazelnuts, followed by hickory nuts, red oak and black oak acorns, then the white oak acorns, and, finally, in late fall and early winter, the walnuts. Squirrels will go for the hickories because they're the first and most abundant early mast, but when the white oaks start to mature, they move straight to them, almost overnight.

If you hunt squirrels on a day-to-day basis, you can stay with the squirrels, but if you only get to hunt once a week or so, they can cut an area out in a matter of days and be gone to another spot. The key is trying to stay with the squirrels as they work the nuts. In large groves of hickories the squirrels may work the area for two or three weeks, but in places with scattered trees, it's a matter of days.

As Brad says, "Here in southwest Missouri where I hunt, hickories are kind of sparse. I might have two or three in one bottom, then another couple over the hill a quarter of a mile away."

Once squirrels are located, however, they'll all be concentrated in one tree or grove of trees, and that's when the cutter call becomes extremely effective. Patience and a bit of cutting will bring even the most wary old bushytail out for a peek at the action.

A wide variety of calls are available, including distress calls to be used in the summer months, cutter calls for fall, and barking calls that can be used anytime.

The Lohman Squirrel Cutter Call consists of a hard, durable, weatherproof striker and a sound peg attached to a barrel. "To use, hold the striking surface firmly," says Brad. "Then take the striker and scrape down the serrated nylon edge of the peg in a fast rhythm. It sounds like a squirrel biting a nut or making the chewing sound as they break the nut. It can be made soft to imitate the sounds made when they cut the softer nuts, such as acorns, by just barely striking the surface. Or you can create the sounds made when they cut the hard nuts like the pig hickories, scaly barks, walnuts, and the like. The squirrels create a lot of volume when they bite into those nuts and the sounds will carry on a still morning for thirty, forty, or fifty yards. Of course, like all game calling, the key is the rhythm, but it's simple; all it takes is a little practice."

Like Brad, I've discovered a great new way to hunt squirrels in the hickories, and one of these days I'm going to beat the squirrels to the nuts again. If I'm lucky I'll find a tree full of squirrels just starting on the delicious nuts, and then I'll be able to have my pie and eat it too.

Winter Bushytails

When deer season comes around most hunters these days pursue venison for the table or a trophy buck. Then, when fall turns to winter, many hunters hang up their guns and pursue other hobbies. But squirrel hunting can be a great winter sport. Since squirrels don't hibernate, winter can offer some great, if not the best, squirrel hunting of the year. Just ask deer hunters, who are often entertained by dozens of squirrels near their deer stand. You also won't have much competition while hunting winter squirrels. In fact, you will probably have the woods to yourself. The weather may be crisp to cold, but it's often better than

Squirrel season is fairly long in many parts of the country, running from early summer through early winter.

fighting the bugs and heat of early-season squirrel hunting. During the late season, squirrels don't have as much pressure from hunters or from non-hunters who simply visit the woods. You also don't have to get up before dawn to hunt. From mid-morning through the middle of the day is often the best time to hunt.

During late season it's important to pay attention to the weather. Cool, crisp days with no wind or rain are the best. Rainy and windy days tend to drive squirrels inside. With the wind and rain, raindrops falling from the trees, and other noises and movements, it's harder for the squirrels to discern predators. During a snowstorm, you'll rarely see squirrels foraging. They usually forage twenty-four hours before and about twenty-four hours after the storm. Wait about a day after a snowstorm and you'll often find lots of squirrels out and about.

Make sure you understand game laws regarding seasons for squirrels. Many states close the squirrel season by the end of December.

Several hunting methods can be used depending on the weather, whether there is snow cover, and the availability of food. Again, one of the most important factors is food availability, which is often concentrated during the winter months. Squirrels have stored nuts in their middens around their nests and tend to stay close to these storage areas. If an agricultural crop, such as corn, is left standing, or has been combined, leaving waste, the squirrels will be on it like kids in candy.

As you can guess by the comment on seeing numerous squirrels from deer stands, one of the most productive methods of winter squirrel hunting is to simply plop your rear down on a convenient stump or log and wait for bushytails to appear. If you happened to see lots of squirrels from your favorite deer stand, simply spend a few hours in your stand. Be sure to take plenty of warm clothes. If you don't have such a deer stand, simply hit the woods and look for squirrels. Of course you should be hunting in places squirrels frequent, such as woods with lots of nut trees. Nuts available in late winter are primarily acorns, along with walnuts. Hedgerows with their Osage orange fruits are favored squirrel wintering areas as well. Creek and river bottoms with their inevitable food supplies are also extremely popular. Watch for dead trees or snags that may harbor squirrel nests. Even small holes in otherwise solid-looking trees may also be a sign of nests. The trick is to move slowly and stop frequently, scanning the distant woods. A good pair of lightweight binoculars can be invaluable for this tactic.

You should also watch for squirrel sign. This can be tracks in the mud or snow. Squirrels bound by placing their forefeet in front of their hind feet, leaving a small four-paw-print grouping every eighteen to twenty-four inches or so. During the winter months a promising sign is small holes dug in the forest floor or around favored nut trees where squirrels have hidden their supply of nuts. Don't make the mistake of hunting leafy nests. Most squirrels have given up these summer homes in favor of the "indoor" comforts of a snug hole in a tree. An abundance of these nests, however, does indicate squirrels living in the area. Even at that, it's not a good idea to shoot into these nests. Even if there is a squirrel in the nest, and you do happen to kill it, you won't retrieve the animal. The squirrel will simply die in the nest—a great waste.

During the early season and through the fall months, squirrels spend the majority of their time in the treetops foraging for nuts and buds. In the winter months they spend more time foraging the ground as they look for dropped nuts and seeds or dig for buried nuts. So watch the ground ahead of you as you stalk.

Fox squirrels are fairly complacent during this time of the year, but grays seem to be more wired than usual. The grays don't stop very long in any one place, but scurry here, there, and everywhere at wide-open speeds. Because they know they're more exposed to predators, all squirrels are extremely quick to find a hidey hole at the slightest sign of danger.

Even though the squirrels are not pressured, stalking them still won't be easy. Wear neutral or camouflage clothing. If snow is on the ground, a snow camo is even more effective. Move extremely slowly. Once I'm in known squirrel woods, or see evidence of squirrel activity, I like to take two or three steps, then lean against a tree or squat down and glass the woods ahead of me. With the leaves off, I can often see a hundred yards or more through the woods. I don't look for squirrels; I look for quick movements. Squirrels always move in quick jumps or darts. Although the flicking of a blue jay's wings or the movement of many of the woodpeckers found in the woods is similar, a bit of time spent watching will reveal the maker of the movement.

Once you spot a squirrel, it's time to make a stalk. Move slowly, carefully, and deliberately toward the foraging squirrel. Keep trees and other obstacles between you and it. Take advantage of terrain, such as ditches, swales, or hills, even if you have to change course. Remember, if you can see the squirrel, it can see you. Be careful of noises. At this time of the year the leaves are often dry, branches and twigs often litter the ground, and it's very easy to make a lot of noise. One trick is to move at the same time the squirrel does. This not only covers your sound, but your movements as well. Get as close to the squirrel as you can before making the shot. Watch it closely. If it flicks its tail and runs to the nearest tree, you may need to make the shot.

Quite often squirrels will scamper up on the nearest limb and then stop to examine the situation. That's the time for a shot, before they head to tall timber, in the top of the tree, and eventually to the safety of their den hole.

Once you spot, shoot at, or shoot a squirrel, stop. Find a comfortable place to sit down and wait. It may take a little time, and patience is definitely a virtue in this game, but you'll probably see other squirrels. Squirrels are notoriously gregarious, and when you find one, you'll usually find others.

Squirrel Hunting Tips

Floating for Bushytails

Squirrels love river and creek bottom lands. The food and cover found in them are usually abundant and lush. One great way of hunting squirrels is to do a float-hunt. Use a canoe, kayak, or even belly boat to float the stream, watching for squirrels foraging the riparian corridor along the stream. It is important to know trespass rules and regulations of the state in which you are hunting. The banks of many streams and rivers are privately owned, even if the stream is public property. In other cases the landowner may own to the center of the stream. Make sure you check with landowners and get permission to hunt both sides of the stream you intend to float hunt.

A canoe makes a great buddy-system type of hunt. The stern person paddles the canoe while the person in the front does the hunting. For safety's sake, the stern person should not shoot. The tactic is simple. Silently glide along, watching the trees overhead as well as vines and fallen trees leading into the water where squirrels will come down to drink. A shotgun loaded with

No. 6 shot is the best choice for this tactic. As with other buddy-system hunts, it's fair to switch positions after retrieving each kill.

Calling Squirrels

Squirrel calls can be extremely effective. Three different types of squirrel calls are available, and it's important to match the calls to the different seasons.

- *Distress Calls*
  Distress calls are made to produce the sounds of young squirrels in distress or being attacked by a hawk, owl, or other predator. These calls are most effective early in the season, or from early summer through late summer. These calls are made in rapid sequence and will often bring squirrels scampering through the treetops from several hundred yards to protect the supposedly distressed young squirrel. These types of calls are normally sucked on, or blown through to produce the high-pitched squealing sounds.

- *Cutting Calls*
  Cutting calls are made to imitate the distinctive sounds squirrels make when using their incisor teeth to cut through the hard outside shells of nuts. I've made them by tapping a quarter against a hard stick. A number of cutting calls are available, but most are a serrated edge over which a hard strike or rock is slowly pulled to create the "clicking" sound. Cutting calls are most productive in the fall months when squirrels are cutting nuts. The sound will often bring several squirrels to investigate where they think another squirrel is feeding.

- *Barking Calls*
  The barking or chattering scolding of squirrels is a sound
  that can be used during any time of the season. This call
  can, however, be easily overused. Squirrels give the call
  when they are alarmed or excited about something. It is
  the common sound many deer hunters hear from their
  stands when Mr. Bushytail discovers someone has invaded
  his territory. Sometimes you can call back and start an ar-
  gument with the squirrel, in which case it may come
  closer to investigate. This is also a good call to use to locate squirrels. Slip into a grove of nut trees, sit down at
  the base of a tree, and wait for about thirty minutes. If you
  don't see squirrel activity, give a barking call. Barking calls
  are normally either a bellows type or a small bulb. In any
  case, rapidly tapping on the call produces the sharp barks.
  The most common tactic is to tap the call four times at
  one-second intervals, and then immediately give a very
  fast eight to ten taps. For best results, listen to the cadence
  of squirrels barking and imitate it. Quite often a squirrel
  will silently slip through the trees to investigate the sound.
      You can also make the barking call sound quite easily
  by using your mouth. With your mouth partially open,
  place your tongue against the roof of your mouth and
  suck it down rapidly, like licking peanut butter off the
  roof of your mouth. The sound is a clicking *kuk-kuk-kuk.*
  Give three or four initial sounds, and then add in the
  eight to ten fast sounds.

The Buddy System

Squirrels are sneaky. When squirrels spot you they simply
sidle around to the opposite side of the tree from you. As you go

around the tree, they also keep moving around the tree to keep it between you and them. It's usually a waste of time to chase them in circles. Two hunters, however, have a great advantage. One hunter can stay still while the other hunter moves around the tree. The squirrel will often slip into sight of the still hunter.

Two hunters, sitting against a tree but watching in opposite directions, can often spot squirrels more quickly than a single hunter. Again, this is also a great way of introducing novices to hunting, including spouses and youngsters. Many a young child has gotten their first taste of hunting sitting under a tree with a parent, grandparent, relative, or friend. It's easy, fun, and pleasant hunting and a great way to spend the day together.

Selling Squirrel Tails

Sheldon's, manufacturer of Mepps fishing lures, purchases squirrel tails to produce their famous fishing spinners. Mepps use squirrel tails because squirrel tails are all hair, with no fur. Practically all other animals have fur tails with just a few guard hairs. Fur doesn't work as well as hair in the water, and it doesn't have the rippling, pulsating movement of squirrel hair. Squirrels are also very plentiful. According to government figures, hunters harvest more than thirty million squirrels each year. Their tails, however, are usually thrown away. This is a waste of a resource. If you hunt squirrels, you may wish to sell the tails or exchange them for Mepps Spinners.

The tails are best on squirrels taken after October 1. Do not remove the bone from the tail, because that reduces the value. Split tails also have no value. Simply salt the butt end of the tail by either generously using dry salt or dipping in a strong saltwater solution. Be sure the tail is straight before drying. Tails that dry curled are useless. Keep the tails away from flies. The best storage place is in a freezer. Do not put the tails in a plastic bag for storage or shipment since they could heat up and spoil. The best time to ship is during the cold months of December, January, February, and March. Send tails to: Sheldon's Inc., 626 Center Street, Antigo, WI 54409–2496. For more information, visit their Web site at www.mepps.com.

Guns and Ammunition

Almost anyone can kill an occasional squirrel with a shotgun, and experienced hunters find it easy to limit out in many areas of the United States. Some early-season squirrel hunters prefer

Favorite guns for squirrels include the venerable .22 with hollow points, as well as shotguns loaded with No. 6 shot.

shotguns when the critters are high in the leafy tree cover and shots are often quick. Almost any shotgun will do, but a 20-gauge is more than adequate. A modified choke is the best choice in chokes. No. 6 shot is the preferred load, with Winchester Super X or Upland Heavy Game Load, Federal Premium High Velocity, and Remington Premier Field loads all good choices.

A real squirrel specialist will prefer the challenge of rifle hunting, and any accurate .22 rimfire will do the trick. There is an art involved, and the difficulties are compounded in the early season when foliage is still thick. This takes skillful stalking and accuracy at ranges from 50 to 150 feet. No boondocks squirrel is ever so trusting as those in city parks or suburban backyards. Let a human appear and these crafty acrobats will immediately scuttle to the far side of a hickory limb and freeze until all danger seems to have passed. Once the quarry is sighted, the specialist seeks the classic head shot. This wastes the least amount of meat and kills the animal quickly and cleanly. Some experts prefer the old-time technique of "barking." The old-time muzzleloader placed a heavy lead ball so close to the head of the squirrel that the concussion killed the animal and not a hair was clipped. These days, most squirrel hunters opt for .22 hollow points, and they are unlikely to kill in this fashion, so pinpoint accuracy is necessary. Carefully placed shots are worth bragging about, and no gourmet meal is damaged.

Traditionalists may use open sights, but many squirrel experts prefer scoped rifles. Although economical small-caliber small game scopes are available for .22 rimfire rifles, the best bet is a quality scope. A number of compact, lightweight, quality scopes are available for rimfire rifles. These often come with the bases needed to fit most rimfires. A better choice is to utilize larger, better quality scopes more commonly used for big game. These offer more power, and more light-gathering power, a definite must when hunting the dark woods of early morning in the early seasons. A 3x-9x variable sighted in at fifty yards can be a tack-driving limit-filler. Variable-power scopes allow you to turn down the power for scanning a tree for squirrels or movement, and then zero in for a tight view. Often squirrels reveal only a tiny portion of their body, and at sixty to seventy feet, it's important to determine what part you're looking at for a quick, clean, and humane kill. The only problem with these higher-powered scopes is that they magnify gun wobble. Make sure you have a solid, steady rest.

A wide range of .22 rimfire ammunition is available from a number of manufacturers. The CCI Mini-Mag is one of the most popular small game loads and is available copper plated. The Stinger hyper-velocity .22 hollow points and Maxi-Mag +V from CCI will handle squirrels, rabbits, groundhogs, and an occasional varmint.

One excellent way of providing for both fast-action and still shots is to hunt with a Savage 24F combination gun. It allows you to match a 20- or 12-gauge shotgun with a rimfire such as a .22 long rifle or .22 hornet.

If you want to add challenge to your squirrel hunting, consider using black powder. A .32 caliber gun such as the Thompson Center Fire Hawk or the Dixie Mountain Rifle in either percussion or flintlock is an excellent choice. Shotgunners can choose from the CVA Trapper, Dixie Shotgun, or the Modern Muzzleloading MK-86, which actually comes with a .50 caliber barrel for big game hunting and an interchangeable shotgun barrel. You can add even more challenge by using a black-powder handgun such as the Colt 1860 Army or CVA 1858 Remington.

Together with venison, buffalo, and waterfowl, America was weaned on squirrels baked or stewed and worked into meat pies. You don't read much about squirrels in the history books, though, because we like to recall our pioneers as center shots on big game.

9

Squirrel Stew, Pot Pie, and Other Goodies

Along with venison, buffalo, waterfowl, wild turkey, and other game, America was brought up on squirrel. Squirrels were boiled, baked, stewed, fried, and made into meat pies. Squirrels are still a traditional table fare for many. This popular small game provides excellent meat that is somewhat like the dark meat of chicken, but with its own distinct flavor. Squirrel meat is somewhat tougher than chicken, especially the meat of older animals. With proper cooking, however, even an older animal can be delicious.

The first step to edible table fare is proper handling of the meat from the moment the animal is killed. During hot weather, many squirrel experts like to field dress or gut the animal as soon as it is collected. This is especially important if a shotgun has been used or if the intestines have been shot. Bacteria from the intestines can quickly spoil the meat in hot weather. Squirrel hair is the biggest problem with dressing squirrels. The hair gets everywhere and is extremely hard to remove from the membranes of the muscles. For that reason many hunters prefer to skin the animal first, and then remove the intestines. This is a good tactic for cool-weather or late-season squirrels.

Squirrels can carry fleas, ticks, and other creepy crawlies. It's a good idea to wear latex gloves when dressing any wild game. Other than gloves, a sharp pocketknife is about all that is needed. A small game holder that suspends the squirrel from a tree limb for dressing can make the chore easier.

Field Dressing Squirrels

To field dress a squirrel, lay the carcass on its back on a solid object such as a stump, log, or rock. Insert the tip of a sharp knife into the skin and just through the belly muscle just forward of the anus. With the knife blade pointed outward, cut up through the belly muscle, being very careful not to cut into the intestines. Holding the squirrel by the back with the other hand can also make it easier to do this chore. When you get to the sternum at the rib cage, continue cutting up through the sternum. Pull the ribs apart, cut through the windpipe and gullet at the throat, and peel the viscera out and downward. Lay the carcass down on a solid surface and, with the knife blade facing downward, cut down through the pelvic bone on the side of the anus. Then scoop out the viscera and cut them off with the anus.

Skinning and Dressing Squirrels

In this method the squirrel is skinned before being eviscerated. Squirrels, especially older ones, are tough to skin and dress. The skin seems to stick like glue. The harder you work the more hair comes off and it all sticks to the meat. My friend Brad Harris, an expert squirrel hunter and Public Relations Director for Lohman Game Calls, says one of the best methods is

During warm weather or before transporting home, squirrels should be field dressed. Or you may prefer to skin, and then eviscerate. A small game holder makes the chore easier.

to skin and dress squirrels underwater. This works especially well if he can find a spring or otherwise safe source of water. Other methods include hanging the squirrel in a game holder, such as those used for other small game skinning; splitting the skin across the back and pulling the two halves off; or an ancient method used by Native Americans and passed on to the settlers and mountain men.

Game Holders

A number of small game holders are available for securing squirrels. The Lohman Game Holder also doubles as a nut cutting call. To dress with a game holder, suspend the holder from a tree limb, other overhead object, or a post at about shoulder height. Holding the squirrel belly out and head down, push its back legs firmly into the holder's outer holding Vs. With the back of the squirrel facing you, cut through the root of the tail, leaving the skin on the top of the tail intact. Then make diagonal cuts from the tail cut around the sides to the belly. Peel this portion of the hide down over the head by pulling downward on the tail and peeling the sides out as you go. Cut off the front feet. You can skin out the head, if you like an old-time delicacy, squirrel brains. Or skin down the neck to the base of the skull.

In either case, the next step is to remove the squirrel from the holder and then reverse the carcass. Place the neck of the squirrel in the center V of the game holder and skin out the remainder of the belly skin and the hindquarters. You may have to use your knife to loosen a flap of skin in order to peel it off. Cut off the rear feet. With the knife blade facing outward, eviscerate by cutting up from the anus through the belly muscle and skin, but not into the entrails. Continue the cut up through the center of the rib cage and into the throat. Cut through the windpipe and gullet, then peel the viscera downward, scraping the liver away from the backbone with your fingertip, or loosen the liver with a knife. Cut down through the center of the aitch or pelvic bone, then spread the pelvis apart and pull the viscera through it. Cut down around the anus to free the viscera.

Split-Skin Skinning Tactics

Squirrels can also be skinned in the same manner as rabbits. Make a two-inch cut through the skin across the back and about halfway between the head and tail. Insert the fingers of each hand under the skin and pull in opposite directions. This peels the fore part of the skin forward and the rear part toward the tail, peeling both sections off. This isn't easy to do, and does take a bit of muscle. With rabbits, it's extremely easy. The skin of squirrels won't tear, however, as will that of rabbits. With the skin pulled over the shoulders and hindquarters and down all four legs, cut off the front and rear feet. Then cut off the head and eviscerate as described previously.

Native American Skinning Method

I learned another method from an uncle, a method that was originally passed down from our Native American relatives. This method is one of the quickest and easiest ways to skin a squirrel, but it does take practice. Once you learn the method, however, you can dress a squirrel in a couple of minutes. Squirrels skin the easiest with this method while the carcass is still fresh and

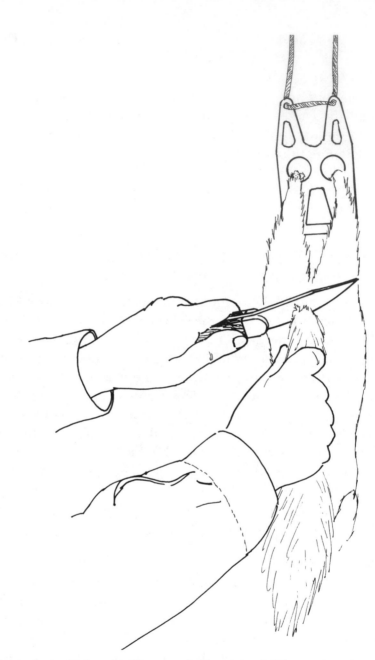

Squirrels can be dressed with a game holder suspended from a tree or post. Push the back legs firmly into the Vs of the holder. Cut through the root of the tail, leaving the skin on the back intact.

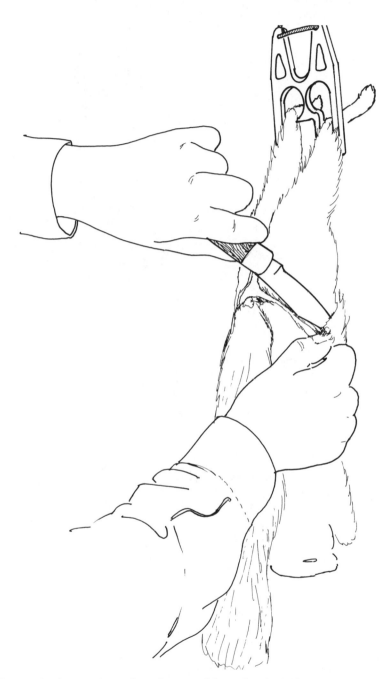

Next, make diagonal cuts from the root of the tail to the belly on both sides.

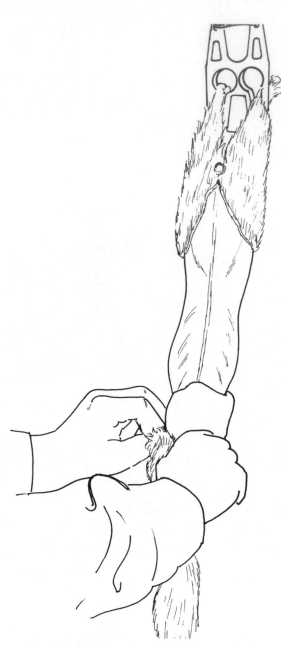

Pull the skin off the back, front legs, and head by pulling downward on the tail. Skin out the head if you want to keep it for squirrel brains or other delicacies.

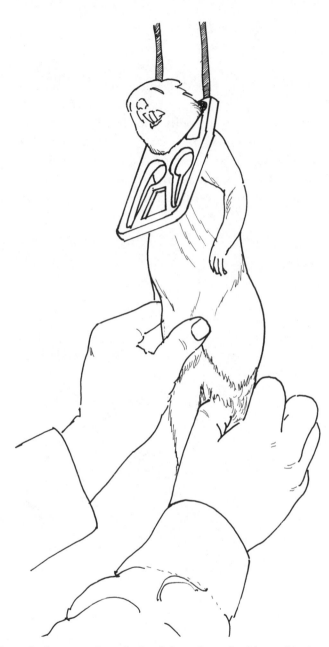

Even if you don't want to keep the head, leave it on the skin at this time. Turn the squirrel upright and hang it by its head in the skinning gambrel. Grasp the skin on the point of the belly and pull down to remove the skin from the back legs.

warm. Cut off the front feet, but leave the rear feet in place for the first step.

Place the squirrel on its belly and, holding the tail with one hand, place your foot on the rear legs. Make a cut across the underside of the tail at the base of the tail. Cut completely through the tailbone, but leave the upper part of the tail skin attached to the body. Be careful not to cut through the tail skin.

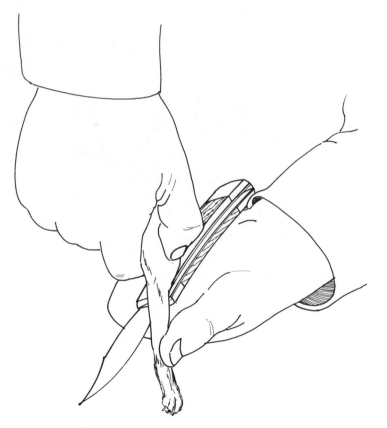

The squirrel can also be eviscerated while hanging in the gambrel. Then cut off the head and feet.

Another method can also be used to skin squirrel. Make a cut through the underside of the tail at the root, leaving the top of the tail skin attached.

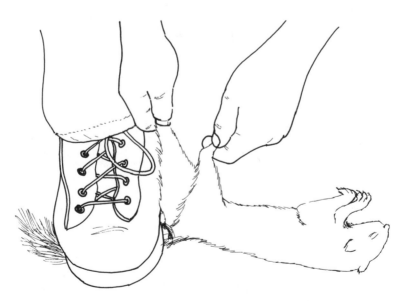

With the squirrel on a solid, flat surface, stand on its tail and grasp the hind legs.

Pulling up on the hind legs will peel the skin away from the majority of the squirrel's front portion.

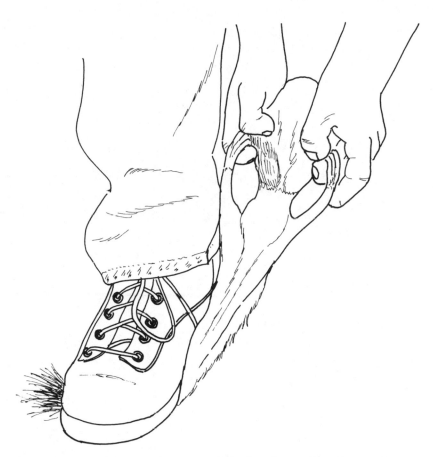

Grasp the squirrel between the head and the front legs and continue peeling until the skin reaches the front feet and head.

Cut off the head and front feet along with the majority of the skin.

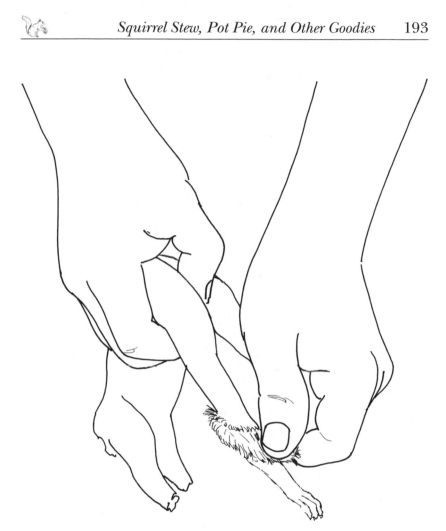

Peel the skin off the rear legs.

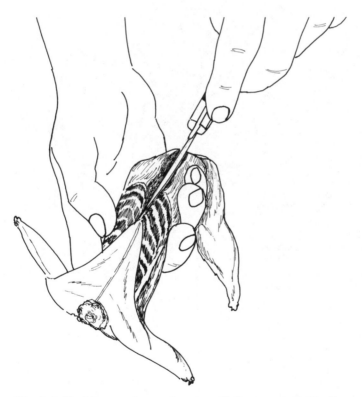

Cut off the feet.

Slit the belly skin, starting at the vent, all the way up to the rib cage, and then cut through the center of the ribcage.

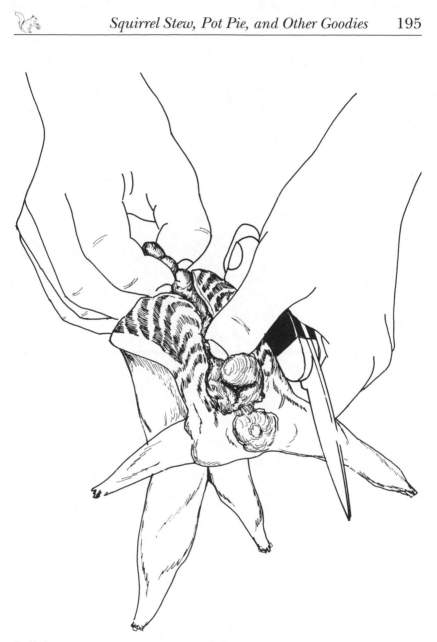

Pull the entrails out and down toward the vent.

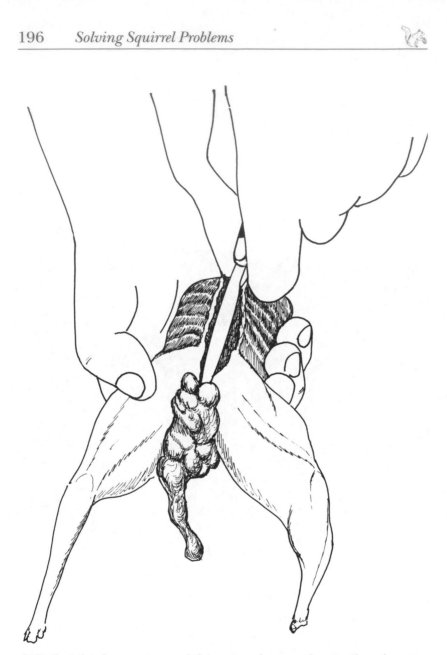

Split the pelvic bone, cut around the vent, and remove the entrails and vent all in one.

Make a cut from this starting cut about an inch or so up the hip of each leg. This cut is somewhat difficult, but easier if you pinch and pull up the skin, then slide the knife underneath the skin with the blade facing upward. This is much easier than attempting to saw through the skin from the outside and also gets less hair on the carcass.

Position the squirrel on a solid surface and place your foot on the underside of its tail. Grasp the hind legs and pull upward. The skin in front of the hind legs will peel off up to the head and over the front legs. Then place your foot on the peeled-down skin section, use a knife to carefully loosen the skin on the belly, and peel it back off the hips and up to the hind feet. Continue peeling the skin over the legs to the feet, cutting them off at the first or ankle joint.

If you don't want the head, cut if off along with the front skin section. If you'd prefer to maintain the head on the carcass, work the skin off the head with short, light strokes, and then remove the eyes. Eviscerate in the same manner as described earlier.

Cleaning and Cutting Up

Regardless of which method you use, and how careful you are, you're going to get some hair on the carcass. Washing the carcass in cold water immediately after skinning can alleviate some of the problem, but you'll probably still end up picking off some hairs, even after a thorough washing. The edge of a knife blade can sometimes be used to scrape away the hairs after the carcass has been soaked in water. Trim off all shot-damaged meat as well as all fat. The fat of most wild animals contains the gamy flavor that some people find unappealing.

Soaking the meat overnight in cold water to which a teaspoon of salt has been added can improve the flavor, especially of older animals. Some cooks prefer to soak the meat in a vinegar and water solution of one part vinegar to three parts water.

Squirrels may be cooked whole, but in most instances they're "quartered" or cut into smaller sections. If you haven't already done so during field dressing, press down on both rear legs with the carcass lying backside down on a solid surface. This dislocates the hip joint. Then cut the rear leg away from the carcass at the dislocated joint. Bend the joint around until you can see the knob of the thighbone and cut around it and between it and the hipbone socket. Repeat this step for the opposite leg. The shoulder is removed by sliding a knife down between the shoulder girdle and the rib cage. Remove the small scent glands located under the forelegs and along the spine in the small of the back. Cut around the glands, but don't cut into them.

If the squirrel is young, these pieces can then be used for frying. This also leaves the back, rib cage, and neck. The larger

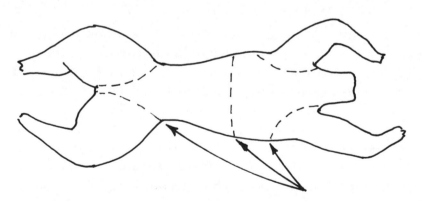

Although squirrels are sometimes cooked whole, they are more often quartered or cut up for cooking.

pieces of meat on each side of the back can be boned out and fried as well. Or you can cut away the back, rib cage, and neck meat and dice it for use in stews or for soup stock. With older animals the entire carcass is commonly used for stews, but it can still be quartered in the same manner. Another method is to place the entire carcass in a pressure cooker and cook according to the recommended pressure and time as specified by your pressure cooker manufacturer. Remove the meat from the bones when it's cooked. You can then grind the meat to make meat salad for sandwiches, or dice it and use it in stews, casseroles, and other dishes.

Transporting Squirrel Meat

Game meat, like any meat, can quickly spoil, especially in hot weather or if simply tossed in the trunk of a vehicle or the back of a truck with heat from the vehicle or sun. Regardless of whether the animal has been field dressed or skinned and dressed in the field, or you intend to wait until you reach home for the task, the meat should be cooled down rapidly. If you intend to skin when you get home and you have a distance to go, it's best to field dress the animal before you head for home. Place the carcass in a cooler with ice, but do not let the meat get down into the melting ice water. One of the best methods is to completely dress and skin the animal, and then place it in a plastic bag on the ice. Or you can simply place the field-dressed but unskinned animals in a plastic bag on ice.

Squirrels should be refrigerated in cold salt water at least twenty-four hours before cooking. They can then be cooked, wrapped in freezer paper, or vacuum packed (the best tactic) using the FoodSaver II from Tilia and then frozen at 0°F for future use.

Aging Squirrel Meat

Before you cook a squirrel, it's important to determine if the squirrel is young or old. Older squirrels can be tougher than your hunting boot, especially if not cooked properly. Young squirrels can be prepared in any number of ways. Smaller squirrels that skin fairly easily are usually the young of the year. The scrotums of older male squirrels tend to be large, blackened, and wrinkled with little hair, while the scrotums of younger males are smaller, smooth, and usually covered with hair. The nipples on older females tend to be prominent and dark; those on younger squirrels are smaller and lighter in color.

Cooking Squirrels

My first experience cooking squirrels didn't turn out too well. While in our early teens, a buddy and I decided to take a "survival" trip. We carried nothing but a borrowed .22, fishing line, hooks, a blanket roll, the inevitable survival kit as described by writers, and a canteen of water. After some arguing with our moms, we headed off into the wilderness—actually a neighbor's woodlot that also held a pretty fair-sized pond. We spent the day turning over rocks to find worms and fishing the pond by hand, throwing the baited hook in the water. We also hunted the woodlot, but weren't very successful. Everything in the woodlot went into hiding with our clumsy attempts at stalking. Then, while sunning on the pond bank, we spotted a big fox squirrel scurrying down a log at the water's edge. A lucky shot and he was ours. It took us the better part of an hour to skin and dress our meal-to-be. By mid-afternoon we were starving and wishing we had brought some of the cookies Mom had just baked. We got a fire started, scraped the scales off a couple of bluegill we had caught, and speared them on tiny green sticks in front of the fire. We then split the squirrel in half and speared him before the fire in the same manner. The bluegills cooked rapidly and we were soon nibbling their succulent white flesh off the blackened skin. Even without salt or any other flavoring, they were delicious. Mr. Squirrel, on the other hand, was getting blacker by the moment. The two bluegills hadn't done much to fill our tummies, so we tore into that squirrel. That was literally how we ate it: tearing it apart with our fingers. Even though black on the outside and red on the inside, we decided it had to be the best-tasting squirrel in the world. We decided we were definitely experienced survivalists ready for more adventures.

Since that day I've learned quite a few ways to cook one of America's favorite small game animals. All of them are tastier than that first attempt. Following are some squirrel and ground-hog recipes you may wish to try.

Soups and Stews

Brunswick Stew

This is an excellent choice for older squirrels that may be tough, although any squirrel meat can be used.

3 squirrels, cut into serving-sized pieces
3 quarts of water
1 cup onion, chopped
¼ cup bacon, diced
2 teaspoons salt
¼ teaspoon black pepper
¼ teaspoon cayenne pepper
2 teaspoons Worcestershire sauce

2 teaspoons granulated sugar

2 1-pound, 3-ounce cans of plum tomatoes, drained

2 cups potatoes, diced

2 cups fresh or frozen corn

2 cups lima beans, fresh, frozen, or canned

Place the squirrels in a large kettle or Dutch oven and cover with the water. Bring the water slowly to a boil, then reduce heat and allow the squirrel to simmer until the meat is tender. This will take from 1¼ to 2 hours. Occasionally skim the broth to remove any fat that accumulates. Take the meat from the broth. After the meat has cooled, remove it from the bones. Then place the meat back in the broth and add the salt, pepper, onion, tomatoes, potatoes, and lima beans. Simmer until the vegetables are tender. This will take from 30 minutes to 1 hour. Add the corn and simmer another 10 to 15 minutes. Stir occasionally to prevent sticking. Pour into soup bowls and serve with cornbread. Makes six to eight servings.

Dutch Oven Squirrel Stew

5 cups boned squirrel meat, cut into bite-sized pieces

½ cup flour

1 teaspoon paprika

1 teaspoon chili powder

2 teaspoons salt

Cooking oil

1 28-ounce can whole tomatoes

2 cups carrots, sliced or diced

2 cups potatoes, diced

2 onions, diced

½ teaspoon dry, crushed red pepper

Mix the flour, chili powder, paprika, and salt and place in a plastic food bag. Place the meat pieces, a few at a time, in the bag and shake to cover. Heat ¼ inch of oil in a large Dutch oven, and then brown the pieces over a medium fire. Add the garlic and onion and cook until transparent. Add the tomatoes and crushed red pepper. Cover the pan and simmer for an hour over a medium fire or until the meat is tender. Add the carrots and potatoes and simmer until the vegetables are tender, another 45 to 60 minutes.

Squirrel Vegetable-Noodle Soup

    1 squirrel
    3 chicken bouillon cubes
    2 quarts water
    4 carrots, sliced or diced
    1 onion, diced
    2 stalks celery, diced
    1 16-ounce can whole or diced tomatoes
    1 can whole kernel corn
    1 can peas
    1 can baby lima beans
    ¼ teaspoon oregano
    1 bay leaf
    2 packages ramen noodles, chicken or picante chicken flavor
    Salt and pepper to taste

Clean the squirrel and place the whole or cut-up squirrel in the water with the chicken bouillon cubes and 1 teaspoon salt. Bring to a boil, then reduce heat and simmer for about 1½ hours or until meat falls from the bones. Remove the squirrel, allow to cool, and then remove the meat from the bones. Cut the meat into bite-sized pieces. Strain the broth, and then add the meat, carrots, celery, onion, and seasonings. Simmer, stirring occasionally, until the vegetables are tender. Remove the bay leaf. Add the canned vegetables, seasoning packets from the noodles, and slightly crushed noodles. Add chicken broth or chicken bouillon and water if more liquid is needed. Simmer until the noodles are tender.

Fried Squirrel

The best squirrel for this recipe is a young, tender one. An older squirrel can be fried, but it must first be parboiled to tenderize it. You can also sprinkle the meat with meat tenderizer before frying. Following are several methods.

Country Fried Squirrel

Soak one cut-up squirrel overnight in salt water. Remove the pieces from the salt water and squeeze them slightly to remove excess water. Pat the pieces dry with paper towels. Roll the pieces in flour and set aside. Melt bacon fat or cooking oil in a deep skillet. There should be enough cooking oil to bubble up around all the pieces. Place the pieces in the hot oil, sprinkling a little salt and pepper over both sides of the pieces before placing them in the liquid. You may also wish to add other seasonings to the pieces as well, such as lemon pepper, herbs, or garlic powder. Fry until the pieces are brown, turning to make sure all sides are evenly browned. Then reduce the heat and cook until tender and the juices run clean when meat is pierced with a fork. If the meat remains tough, add a cup of water, cover the skillet with a tight lid, and cook until the water cooks away. If the outsides of the pieces are soft and sticky, remove the lid and cook a few minutes longer to crisp up the outsides.

Italian Dressing Fried Squirrel

Marinate the cut-up squirrel pieces overnight in Italian salad dressing or your favorite vinegar-and-oil or vinaigrette dressing. Drain the pieces but do not pat them dry. Place flour, salt, and pepper along with your favorite seasonings in a paper or plastic bag. Add the pieces of squirrel, a few at a time, to the seasoned flour in the bag and shake to coat thoroughly. Pour about ½ inch of oil or grease in a deep, cast-iron skillet and heat. Brown the pieces quickly on all sides, then turn down the heat and cook until the juices run clear and the meat forks tender. Remove the pieces from the skillet and make a gravy of flour and water from the pan drippings.

Deep-Fried Squirrel

Squirrel can also be deep fried in a fish fryer or other deep fryer. This method flash fries the meat and keeps all the juices inside for even more tenderness. Cut the squirrel meat into "fingers" or small serving-sized pieces. Pat dry and dip each piece in evaporated milk, then into flour that is seasoned with salt and pepper. For an extra crispy coating, place the dipped pieces on waxed-paper-lined trays. Place the filled trays in the refrigerator for about a half an hour. Then dip and flour each piece again. For an even more crispy coating, repeat the step. Then fry the pieces a few at a time in an outdoor fish cooker or fryer.

Oven Fried Squirrel

2 young squirrels, cut into serving-sized pieces
¼ cup cooking oil
¼ cup margarine
¾ cup flour

1 cup corn flakes crumbs
1 tablespoon salt
½ teaspoon pepper

Cut the squirrels into quarters by cutting off both front and rear legs. Then split the backs down the middle or saddle and cut these pieces into two pieces, producing four back pieces. Roll or smash the cornflakes into crumbs. Place the crushed cornflakes, flour, salt, and pepper in a plastic food bag. Melt the margarine and mix with the cooking oil in a large pan or oven-proof baking dish. The pan or dish should be large enough for one layer of squirrel pieces. Pat dry the squirrel pieces, then dip each in the margarine/oil mixture to coat all sides. Place a few of the squirrel pieces at a time in the bag and shake. Remove the pieces from the bag and place in the baking dish. Bake in an oven for approximately 1 hour at 350°F or until the pieces turn a golden brown, the meat forks tender, and the juices run clear. Serves four. Gravy can be made from the pan drippings.

Baked Squirrel

Bacon and Apple Squirrel

4 to 6 squirrels cut into serving pieces
½ pound bacon
2 ripe apples
1 teaspoon salt
¼ teaspoon pepper
Basil leaves, crushed

Cut the squirrels into eight pieces each, including four legs and cutting the back into four pieces. Place the squirrels in a large, deep baking dish. Do not crowd the squirrel pieces in the dish. Add just enough water to the dish to cover the sides of the pieces. Peel and slice the apples and lay the slices between the pieces. Salt, pepper, and sprinkle with basil leaves. Cut the bacon strips and place over each piece of squirrel. Cover the dish and bake for 45 minutes at 275°F. Then bake for 1 hour at 325°F. Add more water or apple juice if needed to keep the dish moist. This dish is particularly good served over rice or noodles.

Oven Barbequed Squirrel

    2 to 3 young squirrels
    ½ cup cooking oil
    1 cup flour
    2 teaspoons Kitchen Bouquet
    1 large onion
    1 cup barbeque sauce
    ½ cup catsup
    1 cup tomato sauce
    ¼ cup brown sugar
    2 tablespoons horseradish
    1 tablespoon cider vinegar
    Salt and pepper

Cut the squirrel into serving-sized pieces. Baste the pieces with Kitchen Bouquet and then roll the pieces in flour. Salt and pepper each piece, then brown the pieces in oil. Remove the browned pieces and place the rest of the ingredients to make the sauce, with the exception of the onion, into the pan and heat to a boil. Place the browned pieces in a deep baking dish. Slice the onion and place over the meat. Pour the sauce over the meat and onion. Bake covered in a 350°F oven for 1 hour or until tender. Remove the cover and continue baking for 15 to 30 minutes.

Baked Squirrel and Gravy

2 to 3 squirrels, cut into serving-sized pieces
1 cup flour
¼ cup salad oil
2 tablespoons margarine
¼ teaspoon pepper
2 teaspoons salt
1 cup onions, chopped
1 cup sour cream
1 cup milk

Cut the squirrel into serving-sized pieces and roll in flour. Heat the oil and margarine in an ovenproof skillet or Dutch oven. Brown the meat on all sides, then remove the squirrel from the skillet and brown the chopped onion until tender. Stir in 1 or 2 tablespoons flour or as needed into the pan drippings, and salt and pepper to taste. Add the milk gradually, stirring constantly to prevent the gravy from sticking, until thickened. Remove the pan from the heat, place the meat in the skillet, and spoon the gravy over the meat. Cover the skillet and bake at 350°F for 1 hour or until the meat forks tender. Remove the meat and place it in a serving dish. Stir the sour cream into the gravy and reheat, but do not boil. Spoon the gravy over the meat and serve with mashed potatoes or over noodles.

Squirrel Casserole

2 cups squirrel meat, de-boned and cut into bite-sized
    pieces
½ cup flour
2 tablespoons cooking oil
2 stalks celery, sliced ¼ inch thick

3 carrots, sliced ¼ inch thick
1 onion, diced
1 10½-ounce can cream of mushroom soup
1 6-ounce can mushroom stems and pieces
2 cups instant rice
1 teaspoon parsley
Salt and pepper to taste

Dredge the meat in the flour, salt, and pepper and brown in oil in a large, ovenproof skillet or Dutch oven. Place 1 to 2 cups of water in the skillet along with the onion, carrots, and celery and salt and pepper. Bring to a boil. Cover and simmer until vegetables and meat are tender. Stir in the instant rice, mushroom soup, mushrooms, and parsley. Mix together thoroughly, place in the oven, and bake for 1 hour or so at 325°F. Or continue cooking over a low heat on the stovetop. Bake or cook until the rice has absorbed the liquid and is tender.

Squash and Squirrel

2 to 3 squirrels
4 to 6 acorn squashes
Margarine
1 bay leaf per squirrel
3 cloves per squirrel
1 teaspoon honey for each acorn squash

Clean the squirrels and place them in a pot of water. Add the cloves and bay leaves, and salt and pepper to taste. Boil the squirrels until the meat is fork tender and comes easily off the bones. Remove the squirrels from the liquid, pick the meat from the bones, and cut into bite-sized pieces. Cut the squashes in half and add 1 teaspoon honey to each half. Cover the squashes with aluminum foil and bake until they are tender. Remove the pulp from the squash shells, and mix in the squirrel meat, adding a little margarine. Place the squash-pulp/squirrel-meat mixture into the squash shells, place in the oven, and reheat for about 20 minutes.

Cider Squirrels

> 2 to 3 squirrels, cut into serving pieces
> Flour
> 2 tablespoons oil
> 1 small garlic clove, chopped
> Pinch of thyme
> 1 cup sweet apple cider
> Salt and pepper to taste

Heat oil in an ovenproof skillet or Dutch oven. Dip squirrel pieces in flour and salt and pepper each piece. Brown squirrel pieces on all sides in the oil. Add the chopped garlic clove, thyme, and ½ cup sweet cider. Cover and bake for 1 hour at 350°F. Add another ½ cup sweet cider, cover, and bake for about 20 minutes more.

Groundhog

Groundhog and Sweet Potatoes

> 1 groundhog
> 6 to 8 sweet potatoes, peeled and cut into chunks
> Salt and pepper to taste

Dress the groundhog, removing as much fat as possible. Be sure to remove the scent glands. Cut the groundhog into serving-sized pieces and soak in salt water in the refrigerator overnight. Parboil the groundhog meat to remove more fat and partially cook the meat. Place the meat in a deep, ovenproof skillet or Dutch oven. Pack sweet potatoes in and around the meat. Salt and pepper to taste, add water, and bake in a moderate oven until the meat is browned and the sweet potatoes are tender.

Groundhog Stew

1 groundhog
½ teaspoon ginger
Salt and pepper to taste
Oil
Flour
1 onion, chopped
5 to 6 carrots, thinly sliced
4 large potatoes, diced
1 can corn
1 can peas

Dress and de-bone the groundhog, dicing the meat into ½-inch chunks. Soak the meat overnight in the refrigerator in salt water with the ginger added. Parboil the meat for ½ hour, discarding the water and draining the meat. Shake the meat with flour, salt, and pepper. Brown the meat in hot oil, add the chopped onion, and cook until transparent. Stir 2 or more tablespoons flour into the pan drippings. In a large saucepan, cook the carrots and potatoes in salted water until tender. Drain the potatoes and carrots, saving some of the liquid. Stir the potatoes, carrots, and canned peas and corn (along with the liquid from the cans) into the meat and onions. Continue to cook over a low heat for ½ hour, adding potato liquid if too thick or cornstarch if too thin.

10

Squirrels, the Good Guys

Ilike squirrels. I find them amusing, amazing, and fascinating—that is, as long as they aren't digging in my yard, stealing my sweet corn, hiding in the attic, or creating other havoc around my yard, garden, or house.

Other folks also enjoy squirrels. Many municipalities, especially those in the West, have imported gray squirrels for their parks. The town of Marionville, Missouri, has a population of white squirrels, and they're the mascots of the town. Washington, D.C., is considered the "Squirrel Capitol" of the world. Many urban and suburban residents delight in having the little creatures around.

If you enjoy their antics, you can attract squirrels to your yard. The simplest method is to put out bird feed, and the squirrels will find it. Or, you can also add squirrel feed or feeders to your backyard. Then use squirrel discouragement tactics as mentioned in previous chapters on your bird feeders. In this way everyone wins, the birds, the squirrels, and you.

A number of commercially made squirrel feeders are available, including several from Wild Birds Forever. The Squirrel Munch Box has a lid that must be opened. It's fun to watch the squirrels open the lid and dig for corn or peanuts. This feeder

One way of controlling problem squirrels at your bird feeder is to feed the squirrels at their own feeder. Many commercial squirrel feeders are available.

will also keep those annoying jays from stealing all the squirrels' peanuts. The copper siding prevents squirrels from chewing the sides. Constructed of durable, kiln-dried inland cedar, the feeder is great for hours of family fun. Also from the company is Squirrels Delight, Metal Squirrel Feeder. All-metal construction stops those chewing squirrels dead in their tricky little tracks. The feeder is easily attached to a post, tree, or fence with a quick-release body for easy filling and cleaning. The feeder features a front window so lazy squirrels can check out the food level as they saunter by. Constructed of durable, green powder-coated steel, the three-quart capacity holds up to four pounds of seed.

Maybe you would prefer to teach your squirrels table manners with the Wild Birds Forever Squirrel Table and Chair. Con-

*Even if you don't have extensive wood-
lands, you can still attract squirrels to
your backyard and keep them from your
bird feeder with their own feeder, such as
the Squirola Feeder shown. (Photo courtesy Birdola Products)*

structed of durable kiln-dried inland cedar, the feeder holds
one ear of dried corn. A similar design is the Three Squirrel
Lounge Chair. This cedar feeder holds one ear of dried corn
and lets your fat, lazy squirrels lounge around and eat their
corn in proper fashion. Now all they need is a TV set and their
favorite soap opera playing.

The Bushy Tail Seed Cake Feeder is designed to hold any of
the Wild Birds Forever seed cake blends or bushytail squirrel

You can utilize the Squirola Big Ol' Kob on spike feeders. One Big Ol' Kob is equal to nine cobs of corn. (Photo courtesy Birdola Products)

cakes securely and attractively. A hinged roof keeps seed cakes safe and lifts up for easy filling. A bottom-perching shelf offers plenty of room to feed. A wood-based feeder has a plastic-coated wire cage for safety.

One of the more unusual squirrel feeders is the Duncraft Squngee Backyard Squirrel Action Feeder. This feeder is actually bungee bumping for squirrels and it is pure entertainment. Squirrels leap up and grasp at two ears of corn suspended two feet above the ground. Once on the feeder, they swing and bob, traveling up to two feet in the air. The lively action continues as long as the squirrel holds onto the feeder. They have fun and so do you. The unit also has a bell that rings to let you know when you have a visitor.

You can also create your own cedar feeders quite easily if you're handy in the workshop. Or you can make simple feeding stations. These can be used in your backyard or even in the woods during the winter and early spring months if natural foods, such

You can also make your own squirrel feeders quite easily.

as acorns or nuts, are scarce. This is a critical time of year for squirrels and the abundance or lack of suitable food makes the difference between good and poor squirrel production in the spring and summer.

You can stock the feeding stations with corn or almost any kind of nuts. Unshelled corn is an excellent feed if you can find it at local feed stores or mills. You can calculate feeding at a rate of three pounds per week per squirrel. To keep the squirrels from carrying away and hoarding the corn, fasten each ear to a spike driven through a board or wired to a tree; or string ears of corn on a wire and anchor to a solid object. Wire baskets or hoppers fastened to a tree can be used, as well as other special feeders. A row of corn bordering a woodlot can be left standing as a natural feeder, or the corn may be placed in shocks at the feeding station. Usually it is more economical to feed corn in the specially constructed feeders. One feeding station per twenty-five acres is sufficient. Once feeding has begun, food should be provided regularly; otherwise a feeding station can cause more harm than the absence of one.

We're fortunate to live with many acres of woods surrounding us, and we manage them to encourage squirrels. Most farms or properties that have some woods can be managed to increase squirrel populations. Some practices provide prompt results; others require several years for effectiveness, but give results that are more lasting as well as economic gains.

All it takes for good squirrel habitat is work and patience. The amount of work needed to start and maintain a squirrel habitat depends on the basic materials at hand. Any woodland having at least fifty to seventy-five mast-producing trees of various kinds—oak, hickory, walnut, elm, maple, mulberry, and so forth—is a squirrel producer. The first objective is to improve the living conditions for these animals and to raise the carrying capacity for squirrels. This means improving both food and cover.

Food

Squirrels are omnivorous. They eat both plant and animal matter, but their primary diet consists of plants. The abundance or scarcity of foods in an area effects the squirrel populations in those areas. Scarcity during population highs often triggers squirrel migrations. Also, food scarcities depress squirrel populations, as the breeders in poor physical shape fail to bear at their normal rate. A shortage of acorns results in small numbers of squirrels the following year. Bumper crops of acorns produce high squirrel populations from well-nourished breeding stock. The key to productivity is having food available throughout the year.

About the time the first litters arrive in late winter, parent squirrels are feeding on the buds and flowers of hardwoods, particularly the elms, maples, oaks, and sweet gums. Except in years following heavy acorn yields, most of the acorns are gone by spring. When spring arrives, squirrels shift to a diet of mushrooms and mulberries. Then in mid-summer, they shift to a diet of the berry crops of bramble fruits, wild cherries, wild strawberries, and then on to the wild plums and wild grapes of early fall.

Corn in the milk stage is readily used during July and August, as are fungi and the leafy parts of herbaceous plants. Some early use of Osage orange hedge balls occurs at that time as well. During the summer, after the mulberries are gone and before the nuts are ready, squirrels tend to forage on the ground more frequently.

Around the middle of August, squirrels begin "cutting" on the mast crops, usually taking hickory nuts first, along with the staple seasonal foods, acorns. Fruits of sugar maples and honey locusts are also eaten at that time. Then the walnuts, pecans, beechnuts, pokeberries, and ripe corn are ready. Where available, squirrels will often feed on the seeds of cypresses and tupelo gums as well as pinecone seeds.

Squirrels depend on acorns and nuts, either as residues or caches to carry them through the winter. Sometimes these foods are gone before the buds are ready in early spring. On some farms, corn tides the squirrels over, but soybeans, wheat, oats, and even leftover apples are popular as well. Fox squirrels, because of their preference for open timber and small woodlots in farm country, use more grain crops than do the gray squirrels. On the other hand, gray squirrels are more dependent on the natural foods. In one week, a squirrel consumes food roughly the same weight as its own weight.

Cover

Cover is habitat that provides protection for squirrels. It might be a hedgerow on the prairie or a dense forest. Regardless, ground cover and a tree canopy are both critical factors in determining quality of cover and the kinds of squirrels inhabiting it. Fox squirrels prefer mature hedgerows, small woodlots with openings in the canopy, and parklike woods and pastures. Little ground cover is needed; in fact, fox squirrels prefer lightly grazed woodlots with open canopies. Gray squirrels prefer the more extensive and densely wooded areas, usually with closed canopies but with good ground cover of herbaceous plants, shrubs, and saplings. A few windfalls of treetops lopped off by woodcutters attract gray squirrels. By nature, this species is more secretive than fox squirrels, and it needs more cover.

Cover also includes specific shelters in the form of leaf nests and tree cavities. Both species use these as shelters from weather as well as predators. Cavities are scarce in timber less than thirty years old, so leaf nests are used for shelter. Cavities become more numerous as timber age increases; also, older trees yield more acorns. Mature and over-mature stands of trees provide the most homes and food for squirrels. This is also one reason fox squirrels in particular are fond of city parks. Leaf nests are cooler in summer and offer respite from the fleas that often infest dens during winter. Leaf nests, however, are not as durable or as safe as dens. Whether the enemy is weather, owls, hawks, or gunners, dens are the safest shelter for squirrels.

A good den may require about ten years to develop from a natural cavity, and it may last ten to fifteen years, sometimes longer. Some species of trees have a tendency to have a higher number of cavities than others. These trees offer the greatest potential for dens, including the oaks, maples, elms, ashes, sweet gums, and tupelo gums. Osage oranges and hickories are examples of trees that are generally sound even when mature and offer very few cavities.

Typical squirrel dens are formed by the self-pruning of trees within the forest stand as lower limbs are shaded, die, and drop off. Decay may begin at these spots before the opening has a chance to heal over. Trees growing in the open are less susceptible to this type of den formation.

Squirrels also need water. Gray squirrels usually nest near open water, yet both species can survive for many days without trips to pools or streams. Succulent foods, snow, frost, and dew

Allowing den trees to develop will provide both cover and food for squirrels.

are other sources of water. Permanent water, however, should be available to squirrels for drought emergencies.

Management

The most effective management of oak-hickory habitat for squirrels is one of restraint; let the trees grow to maturity. The speed in which squirrel habitat develops and the degree of success attained depend upon overall objectives, perseverance, and the use of special techniques such as nest boxes.

Short-Term Management

One of the quickest ways of attracting and helping squirrels is to provide additional dens. Dens can be built from rough lumber, sawmill slabs, or small hollow logs cut in sections. Mini-

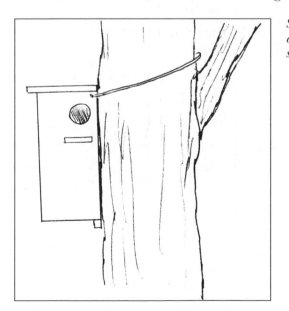

Squirrel den boxes can also be used to help attract squirrels.

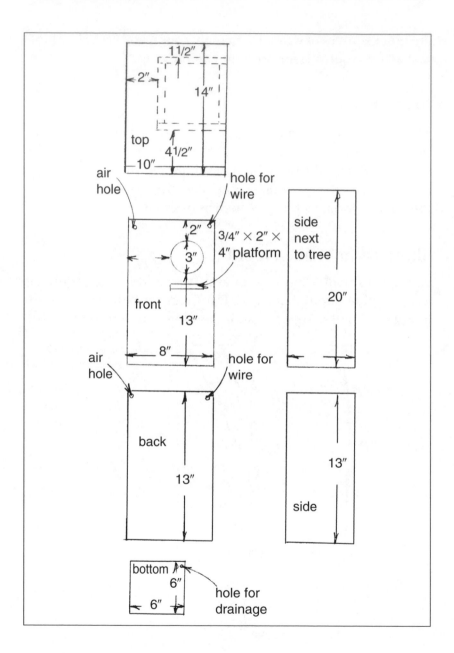

mum specifications for boxes should be followed to assure squirrels will use the den. The length should be twenty inches, and the width should be six inches. The entrance hole should be exactly three inches in diameter and about two inches from the top of the den box. The top must be weatherproof with a front overhang of about four inches. The bottom of the nest box should have a small hole in one corner for drainage. Shown are plans for constructing a wooden den box.

Fill the den boxes about halfway with dry wood shavings or sawdust as a nest starter. Allow three dens for each family of squirrels, but use only one den per tree. The trees should be spaced several yards apart. Use trees that do not have natural dens. Fasten the den against the tree trunk about fifteen to thirty feet above the ground, with the entrance next to a limb or the trunk for accessibility. Use soft, heavy wire instead of nails to fasten the dens to the trees.

Long-Term Management

A long-term management program consists of timber management for both food and shelter. Trees yield better if provided with sufficient space to grow. The following is a good rule of thumb in looking over your timber: The number of feet in the crown diameter of the tree should be roughly twice the number of inches of the diameter of the tree trunk. To achieve this desirable ratio, it may be necessary to thin the stand of trees or make a light commercial cut.

Use the axe and the saw to create better squirrel habitat. Solid stands of even-aged timber can be improved for squirrels by cutting an occasional tree to open up the solid canopy and allow seedlings to grow. This encourages different species of trees and promotes the growth of uneven-aged stands, insuring a more dependable food supply and den development. Squirrels and timber can be grown in the same woodlot by practices beneficial to both. Some trees having no commercial value as saw timber are important to squirrcls, and should be allowed growing space. These trees include mulberries, wild cherries, elms, maples, hackberries, sweet gums, and ashes. Most of these trees not only provide food, but also develop den cavities more rapidly than do some of the commercial hardwoods, and these trees are also useful as fuel.

An average of one elm or maple, one mulberry, and about six hickory trees per acre, along with the oak trees, provides a stable food source, particularly if the oaks are evenly divided as a group. Acorns of the white oak group mature in one year; those of the black oak require two growing seasons.

Managing woodlands for wildlife can benefit squirrels.

A lush undergrowth of hazelnut, hawthorn, dogwood, red-bud, brambles, and wild grape is also desirable. Windfalls or downed trees help create ground cover, which is necessary if gray squirrels are desired. A protective strip of low cover, such as brambles, sumac, hazelnut, and mixed saplings, bordering the edge of the timber keeps down wind movement on the forest floor. This low cover reduces evaporation and temperature extremes, and promotes the growth of forest plants. Woodlot borders can be improved by cutting a strip of timber and allowing it to regenerate naturally. Field borders can be improved by planting a variety of shrubs in clumps or strips. Cattle must be excluded from these areas.

Another method of creating more food and shelter is by the management of the "wolf" trees. These are trees with large spreading crowns that dominate the nearby trees and are objectionable to foresters in timber management. Rather than felling these commercially unprofitable trees, however, they can be girdled and allowed to stand. As these girdled trees die, they often provide dens for several years before they fall, and then the openings in the forest canopy permit other beneficial plants to grow.

The last step is to plant berries, shrubs, and trees that produce squirrel foods. This takes several years to produce results, but once natural production gets going, food supplies are fairly permanent. The greater the variety of plants, the more dependable the food supply, and the more stable the squirrel population.

Sources

Many items mentioned are available from Wal-Mart, Lowe's, Home Depot, and from most of the garden catalogues and gardening Web sites.

Aspects, Inc.
888-ASPECTS
www.birdfeeding.com

Backyard Wildlife Refuge
817-602-8037
www.backyardwildlife.com

Biocontrol Network
800-441-2847
www.biconet.com

Birdola Products
800-BIRDOLA
www.birdola.com

A Bird's World
877-725-1965
www.abirdsworld.com

Bird Watchers Wild Bird Products
800-981-2473
www.birdwatchers.com

Deerbusters
888–422-DEER
www.deerbusters.com

Do It Yourself Pest Control
800-476-3368
www.doyourownpestcontrol.com

Droll Yankees, Inc.
800-352-9164
www.drollyankees.com

Duncraft
800-593-5656
www.duncraft.com

e-Bug Products
800-226-8370
www.e-bug.net

Erva
800-342-3782
www.erva.com

FoodSaver II
Tilia, Inc.
800-777-5452
www.foodsaver.com, www.tilia.com

Havahart & Victor, Woodstream Corp.
800-800-1819
www.havahart.com

Homestead, Gardner Equipment Co.
800-393-0333

Kage-All Live Cage Traps, Kness Mfg. Co., Inc.
800-247-5062
www.kness.com

Kencove Farm Fence, Inc.
800-KENCOVE
www.kencove.com, www.fence-electric.com

Ketch-All Company
877-538-2425
www.ketch-all.com

Lee Valley Tools, Ltd.
800-267-8735
www.leevalley.com

Molechaser, Tower International
800-955-8352
www.molechaser.com

Nixalite of America, Inc. (STUF-FIT)
800-624-1189
www.nixalite.com

Northern Tool & Equipment Co.
800-533-5545
www.northerntool.com

Perky-Pet Products Co.
303-751-9000
www.perky-pet.com

Rid-A-Critter, Dr. T's Nature Products
800–299-NATURE
www.animalrepellents.com

RodentControl-Supplies
877-800-6884
www.rodentcontrol-supplies.com

Safeguard Products, Inc.
800-433-1819
www.safeguardproducts.com

Squirrel Away, Scrypton Systems, Inc.
410-268-9609
www.scrypton.com

The Backyard Bird Store
www.thebackyardbirdstore.com

Tomahawk Live Traps
800-272-8727
www.livetrap.com

Tru-Catch Traps, Heart of the Earth Marketing
800-526-1644
www.animal-traps.com

U-Spray, Inc.
800-877-7290
www.bugspray.com

Whatever Works
800–49-WORKS
www.whateverworks.com

Wild Bird Habitat Store
800-606-2553
www.wildbirdhabitatstore.com

Wild Birds Forever
800–459-BIRD
www.birdsforever.com

Wild Birds Unlimited, Inc.
800-326-4928
www.wbu.com

Index

A

Absolute II Bird Feeder, 55
Absolute II Squirrel Proof
    Feeder, 55
Air-conditioning pipe openings,
    104
Air guns
    for pest control, 131
Albert's squirrel *(Sciurus aberti)*,
    13–14
    range, 14
All-natural repellent, 63
Ammunition
    squirrel hunting, 174–177
Anatomy, 25–27
Animal barriers
    creating, 72–73
Animal repellents, 69–72
Anti-bird nets, 90–92
Apple trees, 87
Apricots, 87
Arboreal squirrels. *See* Tree
    squirrels *(Sciuridae)*
Arizona gray *(Sciurus arizonensis)*,
    3
Attic, 94

B

Bacon and Apple Squirrel,
    206–207
Baffle, 38–40, 95
    commercial, 39
    variety, 39
Bait
    live traps, 140–141
Bait stations, 116, 117–118

Baked squirrel, 206–210
Baked Squirrel and Gravy, 208
Barking calls
    for hunting squirrels, 172
Barn rat, 108
Barns, 93–106
Barriers
    orchards, 90–92
    outside rodents, 120
B-7 Domed Cage feeder, 50
Beehives
    skunks, 127
Big-Eye balloons, 79
Big Top, 48
Bird(s)
    disposing of dead, 59
    watering devices, 60
Birdbath waterers, 81
Bird feeder(s)
    add squirrel resistance, 46–47
    commercial, 43
    discouragement tactics, 36–41
    do-it-yourself feeders, 42–43
    domed bird feeder, 47
    electrifying situation, 41–42
    electronic feeders, 56
    food for, 218
    fruit in, 58
    Havahart, 48
    Haven, 49
    house window feeder, 45
    keeping clean, 59
    location suggestion, 36
    manufactured squirrel-
        resistant, 48
    plans, 44–46

Bird feeder(s) *(continued)*
  platform feeders, 54
  squirrel-proof
    Erva, 55
  support, 38
  tube-style feeders, 50
  website, 53, 229–233
  weight-sensitive feeding
      platforms, 51–52
Bird feeder raiders, 35–65
Birdhouse
  plan, 61
  predators, 62
  protecting, 60–61
Birdseed Vault, 55
Bird Watcher's Marketplace, 55
BirdWatchers Wild Bird
    Products, 56
Bites, 34
Black fox squirrels, 7–8
Black Hole Gopher Trap, 125
Black-powder handgun
  squirrel hunting, 176–177
Black rat, 108
Blueberry patch, 89
Bobcats, 28
Botfly larva, 33
Botta's pocket gopher, 125
Bottom-perching shelf, 216
Box trap, 146–150
  building, 147–150
    materials, 147
Brunswick Stew, 201–202
Buddy system
  for hunting squirrels, 172–173
Bushy Tail Seed Cake Feeder, 215

C
Cages of hardware cloth
  protect individual plants, 72–73
Cage traps
  types, 138
  using, 139–140
California gray *(Sciurus griseus)*, 3
Calling
  Lohman Squirrel Call, 161
  Lohman Squirrel Cutter Call,
      163, 165
  for squirrel hunting, 162, 164,
      171–172
Canoe
  and squirrel hunting, 170–171
Carbon monoxide gas, 85
Catchpoles, 150–152
Cat squirrels. *See* Eastern gray
      (Sciurus carolinensis)
Cayenne, 70
CCI Blazer ammunition, 132
CCI Mini-Mag
  squirrel hunting, 176
CCI pellets, 132–134
Cedar feeders
  create your own, 216–218
Center Fire Hawk
  squirrel hunting, 176
Centerfire shotshells, 132–134
Cherries, 89
Chickaree squirrel, 3
Chimney, 97, 98
Chimney cap, 97
Chipmunks *(Tamias)*, 2, 29–33
  litter size, 29
Cider Squirrels, 210

Clam shell-type live traps, 139
Cleaning and cutting up
    squirrels, 197
Clothing
    for hunting squirrels, 169
CMJ15G feeder, 51
Colt 1860 Army
    squirrel hunting, 177
Commercial tree wraps and
        plastic guards, 126
Communication, 26–27
Companies
    phone numbers and websites,
        229–233
Concealment
    live traps, 141–142
Conibear 55 bodygripper traps,
        135
Conibear 110 bodygripper traps,
        135
Cooking squirrels, 200–211
Country fried squirrel, 204
Cover
    for squirrels, 220–223
Coyotes, 28
Coyote Urine, 69
Create-a-Haven, 55
Cutting calls
    for hunting squirrels, 171
CVA 1858 Remington
    squirrel hunting, 177
CVA Trapper
    squirrel hunting, 176

D
Deep-fried squirrel, 205

Deer mice, 118
Deluxe Squirrel Proof Feeder
    web site, 51–52
Den
    for squirrels, 221
Den development
    for squirrels, 223–227
Diggers
    deterring, 78
Diphacinone, 117
Distress calls
    for hunting squirrels, 171
Dixie Mountain Rifle
    squirrel hunting, 176
Dixie Shotgun
    squirrel hunting, 176
Dog
    tactics for keeping squirrels
        out, 82–84
Do-it-yourself feeders, 42–43
Domed bird feeder, 47
Double-door traps, 138
Douglas squirrel *(Tamiasciurus
        douglasii)*, 11–12
    physical characteristics, 11
    range, 12
Downspouts, 99
Dr. T's repellent, 104
Dressing
    squirrels, 180–182
        illustrated, 184–196
Droll Yankee Flipper, 51
Droll Yankee Giant Seed Tray,
        54
Droll Yankees, 48
    tube-style feeders, 50

Droll Yankees Thistle Domed
  Cage Feeder, 51
Droppings, 23–24
Duncraft Metal Haven Wild Bird
  Feeder, 49
Duncraft Squirrel Blocker
  Squirrel Proof Platform
  Feeder
  platform feeders, 54
Duncraft Squngee Backyard
  Squirrel Action Feeder,
  216
Dutch Oven Squirrel Stew,
  202–203

E
Eastern chipmunk *(Tamias
  striatus)*, 31
Eastern gray *(Sciurus carolinensis)*,
  3
  food source, 7, 21
  gestation, 19
  habitat, 5
  life expectancy, 7
  mating, 19
  physical characteristics, 4–7
  range, 6
Eaves
  examination, 100
Electric fence, 41, 75–78
  charger, 41–42
Electrocution traps, 136
Electronic feeders, 56
Entry location
  house
    examination, 98–104

Erva
  squirrel-proof feeders, 55
Eutamias minimus, 32

F
Fall squirrels
  hunting, 161–165
Families
  squirrel, 2
Fascia board, 100
Feeders. *See also* Bird feeder(s)
  add squirrel resistance, 46–47
  fruit in, 58
  squirrel-proof
    Erva, 55
  squirrel-resistant, 42
  window bird, 55
Feeding stations
  food for, 218
Feeding tips, 56
Feet, 27
Fenced garden, 74–75
Field dressing squirrels, 180
Finch feeder
  squirrel-resistant, 43
Finch feeders, 49. *See also* Bird
    feeder(s)
Fleas, 33
Flicking tail, 27
Floating for bushytails, 170–171
Flowers, 67–85
Flues, 97
Flying squirrels *(Glaucomys)*, 2, 3,
  14–21
Follow-the-mast squirrel tactic,
  161

Food
  fox squirrels *(Sciurus niger),* 8,
    21
  gray squirrels, 7, 21
  red *(Tamiasciurus hudsonicus)*
    range, 10
  squirrels, 219–220, 223–227
  tree squirrels *(Sciuridae),* 3,
    21–23
Food plots
  suited to wildlife, 68
FoodSaver II, 199
4-The-Birds Gel Repellent, 62
Fox and gray squirrels
  food source, 21
Foxes, 28
Fox squirrel *(Sciurus niger),* 3,
    7–9, 169
  food source, 8
  habitat, 8
  physical characteristics, 7
  range, 9
Franklin's ground squirrel
    (Spermophilus frankilinii),
    30
Fried squirrel, 204–206
Fruit in feeders, 58
Fruits, 87
Fumarin, 117
Fumigating gas, 84

G
Game holders, 182–183
Game meat
  transporting, 199
Gardens, 67–85

Gas cartridges, 84
Get Away, 63, 71
Glaucomys, 2, 3, 14–21
Glaucomys sabrinus, 17
Glaucomys volans, 15–16
Gnawing, 23–24
Gopher(s), 123, 125
Gopher Gasser, 125
Gopher Purge Repellent, 125
Gopher repellents, 123
  Mole-Gopher Repellent, 125
Gray squirrels. *See* Eastern gray
    (Sciurus carolinensis)
Great horned owls, 28, 80
Ground-based watering pools, 81
Ground feeder, 47. *See also* Bird
    feeder(s)
Groundhog(s). *See also*
    Woodchuck *(Marmota
    monax)*
  controlling, 84
  damage, 106
  recipes, 210–211
Groundhog and Sweet Potatoes,
    210–211
Groundhog Stew, 211
Ground red pepper, 70
Ground squirrels *(Spermophilus),*
    2, 29–33
  litter size, 29
Guns
  Dixie Shotgun, 176
  pellet and BB guns, 131
  pest control
    air guns, 131
  rimfire rifles, 175–176

Guns *(continued)*
squirrel eradication, 129–134
squirrel hunting, 174–177
black-powder handgun,
176–177
Dixie Shotgun, 176
rimfire rifles, 175–176
Savage 24F combination
gun, 176
type for, 163
Gutter guards, 99
Gutters, 99

H
Habitat
for squirrels, 220–223
Habits
understanding, 1–34
Hand-baiting mouse runs, 122
Hanging peanut butter feeders,
58
Hanging suet feeders, 58
Hardware cloth, 75
cages, 72–73
protect individual plants,
72–73
flowerbeds, 79
Harris, Brad
on dressing squirrels, 180–182
on hunting squirrels,
156–157
Havahart
bird feeder, 48
repellent, 63
Havahart Infinite Feeding
System, 50

Havahart Liquid Squirrel
Repellent, 71
Haven bird feeders, 49
Hawks, 28
Hearing, 25
Hickory nuts
and fall hunting, 161
Hinged perch, 46
Holes
patching, 101–102
Homebrew repellents, 71
Home-built traps, 146–150
Hot pepper spray
create your own, 70
Hot-wire bird feeder
support post, 41
House(s), 93–106
examination, 98
rodent proofing, 111
House mouse *(Mus musculus)*
gestation, 107–109
House rat, 108
House sparrows
shooting, 131
House window feeder, 45
House work, 98–104
Hunting
barking calls, 172
black-powder handgun,
176–177
buddy system, 172–173
canoe, 170–171
Center Fire Hawk, 176
Dixie Mountain Rifle, 176
fall squirrels, 161–165
gun type, 163

Modern Muzzleloading MK-86, 176
muzzleloader, 175
and nuts, 163
squirrels, 153–177
still/stalk, 157
stop-and-go, 157
summer squirrels, 155–160
technique, 157–160
winter squirrels
method, 167
Hunting tips, 170–173

I

Internal parasites, 34
Italian Dressing Fried Squirrel, 205

K

Kaibab squirrel, 4
Kaibab tassel-eared squirrel *(Sciurus aberti kaibabensis)*, 14
Kencove
electric chargers, 76–77
Ketch-All extension pole, 152
Ketch-All Pole
Ketch-All Company, 150
Kill trapping, 134

L

Lawns, 67–85
Least chipmunk *(Eutamias minimus)*, 32
Lee Valley Tools Ltd., 72
Lethal *vs.* nonlethal, 129–152

Lice, 33
Litter size
chipmunks *(Tamias)*, 29
tree squirrels, 3
Live trapping, 137–143
possums, 128
rabbits, 126
raccoons, 128
and relocation, 135, 138
secure, 140
skunks, 127
types, 137–138
Lohman Mr. B's Distress Squirrel Whistle, 157
Lohman Squirrel Call, 161
Lohman Squirrel Cutter Call, 163, 165
Long-term management
to create better squirrel habitat, 225–227

M

Management
to create better squirrel habitat, 225–227
of oak-hickory habitat for squirrels, 223–227
woodlands for wildlife, 223
Mandarin Sky Cafe, 55
Mange, 33
Manufactured squirrel-resistant bird feeders, 48
Manufacturers
phone numbers and websites, 229–233
Marmota, 2, 29–33

Marmota flaviventris, 32
Marmota monax, 32–33
Marmots *(Marmota),* 2, 29–33
    litter size, 29
Martins, 28
Maxi-Mag +V
    squirrel hunting, 176
Meadow mice, 118
Meadow voles, 118
Mice, 107–109
    discouraging, 112–113
    getting rid of, 113–119
Mites, 33
Modern Muzzleloading MK-86
    squirrel hunting, 176
Mole and gopher repellents, 123
Mole-Gopher Repellent, 125
Moles, 122–125
Molt, 25
Motion-activated water sprayer,
    72
Mus musculus
    gestation, 107–109
Muzzleloader
    hunting squirrels, 175

N
Native American skinning
        method, 183–197
Natural predators, 28
Nayarit squirrel *(Sciurus
        nayaritensis),* 12
Nicotine sulfate, 70
Niger thistle feeder with tray, 57
Nixalite, 63, 64
Nixalite's STUF-FIT, 101–102

Northern flying squirrel
        (Glaucomys sabrinus), 17
    range, 17
Northern pocket gopher, 125
Norway rat *(Rattus norvegius),*
        108–109
Nuts
    and hunting squirrels, 163
Nut trees, 88

O
Omnivorous, 29
Orchards, 87–92
    squirrel barriers, 90–92
Organizations
    phone numbers and websites,
        229–233
Outbuildings, 93–106
    rodent proofing, 111
Outside rodents, 118–122
    barriers, 120
    rodenticides, 121–122
    trapping, 121
Oven Barbequed Squirrel, 207
Oven fried squirrel, 205–206
Overhanging branches, 94
Owl scarecrows, 80, 89

P
Parasites, 33
Peaches, 87
Peanut Selective Haven, 55
Pear trees, 87
Pecan Paste
    U-Spray, Inc., 136
Pellet and BB guns, 131

Perky-Pet feeder, 53
Perky-Pet Squirrel-Be-Gone
models, 55
Physical characteristics, 25
Pine squirrel, 3
Pipes
closing openings around,
103
Pival, 117
Plains pocket gopher, 125
Plant protection
cages of hardware cloth, 72–73
Plastic pipe baffle, 96
Platform feeder(s), 47, 54–55.
See also Bird feeder(s)
with corn, 57
Duncraft Squirrel Blocker
Squirrel Proof Platform
Feeder, 54
with millet, 57
with peanuts, 57
PMP, 117
Pocket gophers (family
Geomyidae), 125
Poisons, 137
to kill mice and rats, 116–118
for moles, 124
Polywire, 41
Portable fencing, 41
Possums, 128
Products
phone numbers and websites,
229–233
Psychoacoustic jamming
principles, 81
Purchased feeders, 43

R
Rabbit horn, 33
Rabbits, 126
Rabies, 34
Raccoons, 28, 128
Raised garden beds, 74
Rats
dead
handling procedure,
115–116
discouraging, 112–113
getting rid of, 113–119
sign, 109
Rattus norvegius, 108–109
Red squirrels *(Tamiasciurus
hudsonicus),* 3, 9–10
habitat, 9–10
physical characteristics, 9–10
range
food source, 10
Relocation, 145
and live trapping, 135, 138
Repeat-catch traps, 139
Repellent(s), 62, 104–106
all-natural, 63
animal repellents, 69–72
commercial, 69
Dr. T's repellent, 104
Gopher Purge Repellent, 125
gopher repellents, 123
Mole-Gopher Repellent,
125
Havahart, 63
Havahart Liquid Squirrel
Repellent, 71
homebrew repellents, 71

Repellent(s) *(continued)*
  mole and gopher repellents,
    123
  Mole-Gopher Repellent, 125
  Rid-A-Critter Squirrel
    Repellent, 70, 104
  Ropel Liquid Repellent, 105
  4-The-Birds Gel Repellent, 62
  ultrasonic repellent systems,
    105
  urine repellent
    capsules, 70
  website, 62, 69
Repellent Guards, 69
Retro Fit Cages, 51
Richardson's ground squirrel
    (Spermophilus richardsonii),
    31
Rid-A-Critter Squirrel Repellent,
    70, 104
Rifles. *See* Guns
Rimfire rifles
  hunting squirrels, 175–176
Rimfire shotshells, 132–134
Road kill, 27
Rock squirrel *(Spermophilus
    variegatus)*, 30–31
Rodenticides, 116
  for orchard and nurseries,
    121–122
  outside rodents, 121–122
Rodent (Rodentia) order, 1
Rodent pests, 107–128
Rodent proofing
  fundamentals, 110–112
  outbuildings, 111

Roof examination, 100
Rooftop trap, 142
Ropel Liquid Repellent, 105
Rowe, Karen, 59
Runway, 124

S
Safety
  shooting rodents, 134
Savage 24F combination gun
    squirrel hunting, 176
Scare tools, 79
Scientific Latin family name, 2
Sciuridae, 2. *See also* Tree squirrels
    (Sciuridae)
Sciurus aberti, 13–14
Sciurus aberti kaibabensis, 14
Sciurus arizonensis, 3
Sciurus carolinensis. See Eastern
    gray *(Sciurus carolinensis)*
Sciurus griseus, 3, 6, 12
Sciurus nayaritensis, 12
Sciurus niger. See Fox squirrel
    (Sciurus niger)
Scoot Squirrel, 63
  Whatever Works Garden &
    Home Pest Control, 71
Scoped rifles
  hunting squirrels, 175
Seasonal squirrel foods, 21–23
Seasons for squirrels
  game laws regarding, 167
Selective Haven, 55
Senses, 24–25
Sewer rat, 108
Sheet metal barriers, 123

Shelter
  for squirrels, 221, 223–227
Shooting. *See also* Hunting
  squirrels, 129–134
Shope's fibroma, 33
Short-term management
  of oak-hickory habitat for
    squirrels, 223–227
Shotguns. *See* Guns
Shrews, 122–125
Single-entrance trap, 138
Skinning
  squirrels, 180–182
    illustrated, 184–196
Skunks, 126–128
  beehives, 127
Small game holder, 181
Small mammals, 126–128
Smell, 24
Smoke 'Em Bombs, 125
Snake-proof
  bird houses, 62
Snakes, 28
Soffits
  examination, 100
Songbird, 59
Soups, 201–204
Southern flying squirrel
    (*Glaucomys volans*), 15–16
  physical characteristics, 15
  range, 16
Spermophilus, 2, 29–33
Spermophilus frankilinii, 30
Spermophilus richardsonii, 31
Spermophilus spilosoma, 30
Spermophilus tridecemlineatus, 29–30

Spermophilus variegatus, 30–31
Split-skin skinning tactics, 183
Spotted ground squirrel
    (*Spermophilus spilosoma*),
    30
Spray Away product
  Havahart, 72
Squash and Squirrel, 209–210
Squirola Big Ol' Kob, 216
Squirola Feeder, 215
Squirrel antics, 65
Squirrel Away, 70
Squirrel Away Bird Food, 63
Squirrel Capitol, 213
Squirrel Casserole, 208–209
Squirrel Chase pouches, 71
Squirrel dangers, 33
Squirrel dens, 221
  boxes, 223–225
  plan, 224
Squirrel feeders
  commercial, 214
  create your own, 216
Squirrel foods
  planting and producing,
    223–227
Squirrel Free Bird Feeder, 49
Squirrel Guard
  Droll Yankees, 51
Squirrel Guard mounts
  Droll Yankee, 54
Squirrel hunting tips, 170–173
Squirrel meat
  aging, 200
  transporting, 199
Squirrel Munch Box, 213

Squirrel predators, 27–28
Squirrel Proof Bird Feeder
    website, 49
Squirrel recipes, 200–211
Squirrel-resistant feeders, 42. *See
    also* Bird feeder(s)
Squirrel-resistant finch feeder, 43
Squirrels
    feeding, 80
    jumping ability, 36
    life expectancy, 28
    trapping, 65
Squirrel season, 166
Squirrel-Selective, 55
Squirrel sign, 23–24, 168
Squirrel tails
    selling, 173–174
Squirrel Vegetable-Noodle Soup,
    203–204
Stalk
    hunting squirrels, 157
Steel traps, 134–136
Stews, 201–204
Still/stalk
    hunting squirrels, 157
Stop-and-go
    hunting squirrels, 157
Stores
    phone numbers and websites,
        229–233
STU-FIT, 101–102
Suet feeders, 56
Summer squirrels
    hunting, 155–160
Sunflower Domed Cage Feeder,
    51

T
Tactile hairs, 25–26
Tails
    selling, 173–174
    website, 174
Tamias, 2, 29–33
Tamiasciurus douglasii, 11–12
Tamiasciurus hudsonicus. See Red
    squirrels *(Tamiasciurus
    hudsonicus)*
Tamias striatus, 31
Tassel-eared squirrel, 4, 13
Teeth, 2–3
4-The-Birds Gel Repellent, 62
Thies, Jerry
    squirrel hunting, 160
Thirteen-lined ground squirrel
    *(Spermophilus
    tridecemlineatus),* 29–30
Thompson/Center Encore .410
    pistol, 132
Three Squirrel Lounge Chair, 215
Ticks, 33
Tilia, 199
Time-release capsules, 70
Toes, 2
Tracks, 23–24
Trap(s)
    checking, 142–143
    phone numbers and websites,
        229–233
Trapped animals
    dangers, 145–146
    releasing, 146
Trappers Choice Coyote Urine,
    69

Trapping
  animals, 143–144
  armadillos, 144
  cottontail rabbits, 144
  designed to kill animal, 134
  muskrats, 144
  outside rodents, 121
  to remove rats and mice,
     113–115
  squirrels, 143
  woodchucks, 144
Tray or platform feeders
  with corn, 57
  with millet, 57
Tree branches
  house, 94
Tree guards
  field mice and cotton rats, 121
Tree squirrels *(Sciuridae)*, 2, 3–21
  feet and claws, 27
  food source, 3, 21–23
  food storage, 20
  habits, 17–21
  litters, 3
  nesting habits, 18
  tails, 26
  varieties, 3–4
Tree work, 94–98
Trimming
  limbs, 90–92
Triple-Bin bird feeder, 47
Tube feeders
  bird, 49
    with black-oil sunflower
      seeds, 57
  with peanuts, 57

Tube-style feeders
  Droll Yankees, 50

U
Ultimate Feeder
  from Havahart, 50
Ultimate Feeding System, 48
Ultrasonic devices, 81
  to deter mice and rats, 113
Ultrasonic repellent systems, 105
Ultrasonic Squirrel Deterrent
  Whatever Works, 82
Ultra Sound Repeller, 82
Urine repellent
  capsules, 70
U-Spray, Inc.
  electrocution devices, 136
Utility lines
  squirrel pathway, 95–96

V
Varicraft Bouncer Squirrel Proof
    Feeder, 55
Vent pipes, 98
Vibrissae, 25–26
Vinyl soffits, 102
Voles, 118

W
Washington, D.C.
  squirrels, 213
Water
  for squirrels, 221
Waterers, 81
Watering devices, 60
Weasels, 28

Weight-sensitive feeders, 51–52
Western gray *(Sciurus griseus)*, 3,
	12
	range, 6
Wharf rat, 108
Whatever Works, 63
Whatever Works Garden &
	Home Pest Control, 49
Whiskers, 25–26
Whistle pigs, 33
Wild Birds Forever, 49
	platform feeders, 54
	squirrel feeders, 213
Wild Birds Forever Squirrel
	Table and Chair, 214–215
Wildlife garden, 67
Window bird feeders, 55
Winter bushytails
	hunting, 165

Wire cylinders
	field mice and cotton rats, 121
Wire guards
	meadow mouse problems, 120
Woodchuck *(Marmota monax)*,
	32–33a
Wooden-based snap trap, 115
Woodlot management, 92

Y
Yankee Flipper, 51
Yard sharks, 122–125
	barriers, 123
	poisons, 124–125
	rodenticides, 124–125
	trapping, 124
Yellow-bellied marmot *(Marmota
	flaviventris)*, 32
Yellow-faced pocket gopher, 125